Motherhood Uncensored

35 Authors Explore Things Left Unsaid About Motherhood

Beverley Pannell

MU
—BOOKS—

Cover design by Nabin Karna.

Published by MU Books, 2025
ISBN: 978-1-0369-0841-6

Motherhood Uncensored: 35 authors explore things left unsaid about motherhood is also available in ebook format.

Profits from the sale of this publication will be shared with Make Birth Better Community Interest Company (CIC) and PND Awareness and Support (PaNDAS Foundation).

Make Birth Better is a unique collective of parents and professionals working together to end suffering from birth trauma through support, campaigning and training. makebirthbetter.org

PaNDAS is the leading UK charity in supporting families suffering from antenatal and postnatal illnesses. PaNDAS' vision is to support every individual suffering with perinatal mental health illnesses, and those within their network. pandasfoundation.org.uk Charity number 1149485

To everyone who has ever wondered
'is it just me?'

It's not.

MOTHERHOOD
UNCENSORED

CONTENTS

Perspective Shifts...179

Afterword... 241

Resources and support 249

Foreword

This is a tear spattered foreword and how could it be anything else? For across the pages of this poignantly honest collection every type of emotion is laid bare and generously shared, by those who are mothers and those who are not (yet) or may never be. But the beauty of the short stories comes from the way they collectively and in different ways, illuminate the hidden, mundane, harrowing, loving, eternal and contradictory contours of maternal experiences, lived, witnessed and silenced across generations: for we have all been mothered. Writing this foreword is a precious thing to be entrusted to do, especially because so many aspects of motherhood are precious, exposing and endured but remain unspoken.

The question of why we can feel silenced and unable to share how we really feel about reproductive and maternal experiences, has been a recurring question in my research for over 25 years. In this I have explored how experiences of motherhood unfold and why this transition and the responsibilities that ensue are largely ignored societally as something unremarkable, something to be got on with, without complaint, something to be borne ('Motherhood: Contemporary Experiences and Generational Change' Cambridge University Press, 2023)

As myths of motherhood as 'natural' and so somehow easy and instinctive continue to be perpetuated, the contributions in this collection cut to the very heart of the matter, shining a light on shared experiences that are visceral and challenging, but most of all, honest. As the inspiration behind motherhood-uncensored.org and this wonderful collection, Beverley Pannell has provided a vital space in which uncensored accounts can be shared, recognising the need to challenge and re-set any agenda on what is 'normal' about mothering and motherhood – and who says. Most aspects of chasing fertility and motherhood are demanding and unexpected and require skill sets that would be prized in other areas of our lives but don't count in the home and are scrutinised by others when out and about in the public sphere.

But it's normal to struggle, to feel lost in the overwhelming emotions that accompany hopes for positive fertility outcomes and everyday mothering, if achieved. As we are jettisoned into new, sometimes longed-for worlds, which are different to what had been 'planned' why wouldn't we feel confused, even if temporarily? But it can be hard to share feelings of not coping or enjoying every detail of life with a baby - or managing loss - especially when it appears that others around you are doing well. In other spheres of our lives, such a key responsibility would attract support and gratitude at the important job being undertaken, selflessly. But instead we are mostly invisible and ignored or in the way, taking up space with baby paraphernalia.

The accounts shared in this collection, which take the reader through fertility journeys, agonising loss and grief, love and issues of mental health and societal injustice, are not the sanitised, airbrushed versions of 'good' motherhood or womanhood. These accounts are the lived, survived, visceral experiences that make up the everydayness of being (or contemplating being) a mother, a parent, with or without the physical presence of a child. Together these pieces produce a rich patchwork of everyday experiences, which reach back into the past and forward as (maternal) futures are imagined. But even with the weight of what it bears, the collection is also celebratory. This is because only by hearing and making visible the contours of all fertility and maternal vulnerabilities and experiences can we know how magnificent and powerful women are, living with the ragged emotional terrain that these experiences can reap. So dear reader, prepare, for it is not an easy ride, but then fertility experiences and motherhood at their most granular level, rarely are: But they deserve to be heard and seen and felt and held. We can do this collectively, witnessing, normalising and celebrating each brave contribution, whilst making a mental note to metaphorically wrap our arms around all women and mothers, for we never know what they may be going through.

Professor Tina Miller
Oxford Brookes University

Introduction

I set up Motherhood Uncensored, the organisation behind this book, to tackle myths, misogyny and nonsense about motherhood. My desire to create space for frank, authentic discussion grew out of my own experience of early motherhood, which seemed wholly disconnected from the image that I'd been sold.

Right from the outset I felt like an outsider. I didn't make my decision to try and conceive the right way: my weighing up of pros and cons was too pragmatic without the requisite reference to ticking clocks and eager ovaries. I didn't feel the right emotions through pregnancy. Losing my first pregnancy at 12 weeks made me braced and fearful throughout the full term of the next one. I wasn't *so excited* or *desperate to meet them*. I was just worried. My body didn't 'just know' how to give birth. When my daughter was born there was no rush of abounding love, just relief for the experience to be over. The buttery toast an hour later will remain the highlight of that day for me. Clearly, my brain thought the wrong way. My body couldn't do what it was supposed to naturally do. I didn't love my baby the way I was supposed to. I was doing everything wrong and felt uniquely unsuited to this new role I had committed to.

It took me months of making tentative connections and wading through a fog of comments like 'oh I wouldn't change it for the world' before I began to see clearly. To see that I wasn't the problem. That I, and in fact all of us, had been set up to fail against expectations that are wildly out of reach.

The motherhood myth is deeply ingrained, and it gets protected by a conspiracy of silence in which too many of us have been complicit.

To some extent we all absorb the myth. We're practically marinated in it from a very early age. If you have a womb then you're told you must, during a tiny acceptable age window, want to grow children in it. Don't do it too young. Don't do it too old. You must conceive those children naturally, holding the pregnancy to term, whilst being joyful and excited throughout. You must birth naturally and calmly and then spontaneously become a fountain of breastmilk, being 'mumsy' and treasuring All Moments. Life will be a montage of Insta-perfect crafting sessions, walks and snuggles, unaffected by all those terrible things that happen to 'other people'. You must put the baby first in all decisions, including those directly affecting your own physical and mental health and then spend the next 20+ years dedicating yourself to them fully, regretting nothing and ideally continuing to earn an income and look 22.

This is the experience of Absolutely No-One.

Perhaps there is a small minority for whom this doesn't feel so far from their lived experience but they are just that- a minority. A blissful one, sure, but a minority nonetheless. Those of us who deal with the gritty bits of life, who aren't always sure, who can countenance the idea of regret, who know loss and fear and disappointment, we are the majority.

The motherhood narrative is ours for the taking.

Our stories are left unsaid because we incorrectly think we're alone. We think everyone else is much closer to the ideal. We think we'll be judged and looked down on if we share our unsaid things. But who can look down on us? The people 'higher up' are only imagined.

And our silence isolates us.

Adrienne Rich in 'Of Woman Born' talks about how 'mothers are divided from each other in homes, tied to their children by compassionate bonds'. Mothers are all doing the same work: mothering. We are conditioned to not see it as work, and to not see ourselves as workers. Rich points out that workers can unionise and strike and that even a forced labourer can 'hate or fear his boss... loathe the toil; dream of revolt'. None of us would consider changing our life for that of a forced labourer but it's easy to see what Rich means when she says:

> 'the woman with children is prey to much more complicated, subversive feelings. Love and anger can exist concurrently; anger at the conditions of motherhood can become translated into anger at the child, along with fear that we are not "loving"; grief at all that we cannot do for our children in a society so inadequate to meet human needs becomes translated into guilt and self-laceration'.

> Adrienne Rich, Of Woman Born

Motherhood as an institution, a set of norms and conventions dictating what's expected, is deeply, dangerously flawed. That makes the experience of motherhood, to dramatically understate it, complicated.

Let's say so.

When we censor ourselves and limit our discussion to the positive we inadvertently censor each other too. We close down the space for honesty. I've been in so many conversations where people have 'asked' me: 'it's wonderful, isn't it?'. The menacing tone to 'isn't it' is barely hidden. These questions tell me the range of answers that will be deemed acceptable, and it's a very limited range indeed.

Is there any other area of life where we are quite so intolerant of nuance? We make big decisions about family, friends, work, where to live, how to live. In all areas we recognise that people have a range of views and experiences and that there are highs, lows, mistakes and regrets. Not with motherhood.

It's easy to see why each of the entries included in this compendium would be left unsaid. Each took courage to write and share. But each describes an experience that is more real and more common than the fairy tale. Each opens a conversation rather than shutting it down. Collectively they make more space for others to say what they've left unsaid.

That's why I wanted to publish this book. Words are powerful. They help us clarify what we think, what is true and who we are. Reading other people's stories and reflections helps us see that we're not as isolated as we thought. I consciously decided to not restrict entries to 'writing by mothers' because unrealistic expectations about motherhood affect everyone. Not just mothers. Not just women. Everyone.

In the pages which follow you will find powerful reflections on motherhood. Stories which tackle love, grief, loss, injustice, fertility, abuse, friendship and family. Inevitably, it's not a light and breezy read. You will find content warnings to guide your reading, but please do go easy on yourself and skip entries that you don't think you're in the right headspace for. There are sources of support listed at the back.

I hope that in reading this collection you find validation of your own thoughts and feelings, solidarity with others and a reminder that we only ever know a tiny fraction of what's going on in each other's lives. Perhaps you'll find a challenge to create more space for these conversations in your own community. Perhaps you'll find the confidence to recognise that you're in the majority, and that you needn't leave things unsaid for fear of the consequences.

I want to thank everyone who supported the competition which launched this book. Hundreds wrote entries and thousands voted to decide which got included here. Evidence, if it were needed, that there is a real hunger to talk about motherhood in a radically different way.

I'm very grateful to Jess and Saveeta, Motherhood Uncensored trustees who offered support, advice and practical help throughout and Hannah at Starcroft Farm Cabins, who partnered with Motherhood Uncensored to run the competition and also offered a retreat at one of her beautiful cabins as part of the prize. Likewise to our competition judge Lucy Jones, author of *'Matrescence: On the Metamorphosis of Pregnancy, Childbirth and Motherhood'*, to literary agent Hannah Sheppard who gave feedback as part of the prize, and to Alex Bollen, author of *'Motherdom:*

Breaking Free from Bad Science and Good Mother Myths' for reviewing the manuscript.

Professor Tina Miller has written extensively on motherhood, the expectations that surround it, and how the lived experience of mothers across generations has fallen short of those expectations. Her most recent book ('Motherhood: Contemporary Experiences and Generational Change' Cambridge University Press, 2023) has won an American Library Association 2024 Choice award for Outstanding Academic Titles. I came across her work when I was in the early stages of launching Motherhood Uncensored and she has been a source of encouragement and guidance throughout- I was delighted that she agreed to write the foreword which sets the tone for this book so eloquently.

I have found these stories inspiring and insightful. Beautifully written, sometimes funny, sometimes heart wrenching, always frank. None of them exactly replicate my particular circumstances or story, and yet in all of them I see kinship. I see people finding hidden depths of strength and compassion when life veered off script. I see people brave enough to stop and think, and hard won wisdom being freely shared. You'll see that too.

Thank you, too, for your support in buying this book and thanks on behalf of Make Birth Better and PANDAS Foundation to whom we're donating a proportion of proceeds.

If you find this book a fraction as valuable as I've found it then you won't be disappointed.

Beverley Pannell
Editor and Founder of Motherhood Uncensored

Winning Entry: To the Undertoads, by Fran Hortop

This piece was chosen by Lucy Jones, author of *Matrescence: On the Metamorphosis of Pregnancy, Childbirth and Motherhood* as the overall winner of the Things Left Unsaid motherhood writing competition.

Content guidance*: infertility, failed fertility treatment and associated grief.*

-

A post-treatment break at the seaside. A walk in the Undercliff, to pace disappointment away through five miles of coastal landslip. A haven for the childless, with small-people-repelling ups and downs, and an outrageous absence of ice cream vendors. The anti-Lyme: for every tourist nick-nack, a thicket; for every postcard vista, a twist of gloom. Family unfriendly. How very comforting.

My one-man family strides ahead, walking sadness into purpose on long legs. We have each other for this adventure, he and I, and a backpack full of healthy snacks, lashings of half-grief and the ghost of a pregnancy to lay to rest. Blister plasters and camera-phones to snap the spaces next to us where our offspring aren't.

I am a lacklustre forest adventurer today. In need of a walk's therapy but body unwilling. I fall behind with the ragtag of shadow sprites that keeps me company wherever I go these days. We track him through darkling paths, crash through trees displaced in his wake. I stumble, snag hair on brambles, yelp; amusement for passing walkers. I hear them laughing at the back of the pack, little ones new to the gang, results of recent medical tinkering: puckish, slithering, carousing little undertoads who walk with me from Lyme to Seaton.

They rush along to the beat of my internal metronome. Rusting, wrong, but faithfully good at keeping monthly time. It won't shut up! Its edges pierce my hidden middle flesh now, ratcheting through me like a medieval torturer's prized contraption, mocking that sublime endgame of womanly pain. This month, especially vigorous, working overtime to expel and cleanse the grade two and three toadpole oocytes that just couldn't get comfy in my perfectly formed, yet hostile womb. Giving me a galumpher's gait, as I clamber over the forest floor, wearing increasingly uncomfortable knickers that won't wash out in a hotel basin.

Hard not to imagine my body hijacked by those toads. They already hold my purpose and identity in their filthy little fists. Keeping me trapped in this obscure wood as friends rush bellylong into motherhood. Spoilsporting walks like this is a wheeze, vile sprites! Now, pulling out all the stops to hobble me. Heaving branches in my path, making my limbs so, so heavy. I try to keep up with my family man, but our toady children merely stalk him while for me it's full-throttle siege and maraud: a mother's privilege and burden? (Because surely, when I am with them, I have a right to that name?)

Ho! Sprites, hang on to my legs now. A snicker from the pack. Let's bring her down, lads! I, pitching forward as they clamber on my back. They, toady fingers twisting my hair, reaching to pinch my cheeks, give breath-sucking kisses, dragging with full might on my arms, nearly socket-free.

Pull me into your toady Undercliff kingdom. I want it. Pull me round the waist, down. I want it.
I can be your eternal Undercliff queen, your nurse, your heart of oak, your mamma. Pluck at my uterus with grubby fingers, like a winsome ukulele to be hurled into the bush when bored. Pluck it out!

****

Our seaside panacea path plunges into civilisation, the world, the Cob, the pub. The toads retreat to plot moves to floor me. We eat nursery-style fish and chips for two while proper families whirl in the official stress of tantrums, toileting accidents. I toast the toads as we drain glasses of their wine and feign delight in another month's freedom of lie-ins, elaborate meals, city breaks. The red spot at the bottom of the glass removed by dishwasher, mirrored on the inside by the spot that comes with magical timing every month. Currently in full flood. Bloody purple, bloody painful, bloody ghastly, the same old bits of proto-baby cell and promise.

I consider this clockwork sorcery in the pub loo, while a child attacks the wall of the next-door booth, and his mother's sing-song cracks as she imagines the worst of what I must be thinking. (Can't she control her child?) His little fists provide the beat to my earworm nursery rhyme about the fate of the barren woman, a backwoods fairy-tale of that recurring red spot, not on her forehead for everyone to see, but worn into her most capacious knickers over the weeks and months. The red of hopes dashed like Riding Hood's brains on a forest boulder. The Disney chorus of dreadful, hollow-eyed toad-sprites calling from sinewed woods. (Can't I control my children?)

I hold my need for a different fate in my hand, along with one more glass of wine, as the hordes of parents around us gather like extras in a zombie movie by the ice-cream kiosk outside. Great meandering phalanxes with their flesh-made offspring, oblivious to my own fleshless figments of desire and biological imagination that hassle and buffet me, so I look unsteady, a childless early evening lush.

Back at the hotel, we all pile into a spacious double ensuite room (with matching bathrobes), where they surf inappropriate TV channels, use up the complimentary bath condiments, soak their toady selves in the family sized bath. Stay up past bedtime to sabotage grown-up conversation. Sit fat and stinky in a draughty seafront breakfast room, not eating their boil-in-a-bag kippers. They don't need highchairs, buggies, plastic distractions, but their un-bodily shapes take up space, nonetheless.

Tomorrow, back to London to insert ourselves into the rush of living. To ruin everyone's week with news of another failed IVF round. To restart the diets, the wellbeing regime. To the counting: of fertility-boosting ingredients in the mega-smoothie; the number of drinks we can have at dinner; the pennies in the bank as we save again for more baby quackery; the number of days until we can try again. A signal for the sprites to rush back to the Undercliff, the toadpoles released into shadow, where they course with brothers and sisters that never were, never to be.

'*Treasure every moment*'

Reflections on early motherhood

Just tired, by Emma Sparks

Shortlisted entry

-

Becoming a mother has made a liar out of me. I can no longer answer the most basic question honestly.

How am I?
How much time do you have?

Some people – often other mums – pair the query with a knowing, earnest look. But they're complicit in this charade. No one wants to hear the truth. Not really. They're hoping there's time for another cuddle or nose boop with my babbling bundle of... Besides, if I share too much they'll start to worry, or worse – cut me off with a sharp invalidation.

Baby's here safe and that's all that matters.
Is it?

So instead I smile. *I'm fine, just tired.*
But what I really mean is...

I'm broken. My bones ache. This is so. fucking. relentless.

Days slip through my fingers, leaving nothing in their wake but a mess, more work to do, more scattered thoughts. Nights loom large; gaping black holes loud with white noise, heart-stopping wake-ups and nerve-jangling cries.

I'm fraying at the edges. Strands of my identity tugged loose and discarded by tiny hands.

My to-do list only ever gets longer, temper shorter, patience thinner. There is no time. There's a reason sleep deprivation is used as a torture technique. My brain plays a frantic inner monologue day and night, pinballing between pointless thoughts, misfiring synapses stuck on repeat.

What have I done?

I forgot to sterilise the pump again.

Look at that gorgeous face.

Shouting near prams in parks should be a crime.

Punishable by death.

Will I ever have sex again?

He's perfect.

We should have got a puppy instead.

Why do my farts smell like the baby's farts?

I thought I was more resilient than this.

I mean it – his don't smell like mine; mine smell like a dirty nappy.

Those eyelashes.

Babies are being blown to pieces in Gaza.

I'm sobbing because mine won't sleep.

Those images will haunt me forever.

I'm so selfish. Egocentric. Weak.

Yes, I probably just need a nap. But please don't tell me to sleep when the baby sleeps.

No one ever told me how hard this would be. And now I know why. Trying to define this divine chaos is nigh on impossible. So we skim over the details, tidy away our traumas, talk about the (abundant) positives and diminish the full spectrum of this experience until we're parroting platitudes rather than telling the truth.

Motherhood can be so shit. But *I wouldn't change it for the world.*

I absolutely would.

If this is a test, I'm failing. It was the same in pregnancy; each intervention proof, in my eyes, that I wasn't enough. They sliced me open, birthed my baby for me because I *failed to progress.*

The problem isn't him, it's me. Perfectionist. Control freak. Productivity addict. These traits don't align well with motherhood. These are the flaws that have floored me. Believe me, I wish I could surrender to the chaos, enjoy each moment, *just relax.* Sometimes, I do.

But sometimes, frazzling fatigue invites self-doubt, paranoia and ferocious rage to test my nervous system further, turning me into a wild wolf mother. Teeth bared. Back up. Howling. Alone. Spikes of anger giving way to cruel self-criticism and endless guilt.

Of course I'm happy. I longed for this. Stabbed needles into my soft flesh night after night for this. Stuck hormone pessaries where the sun doesn't shine for months for this. Endured sickness and stress and surgery. All for this.

Of course he's worth it. I have never known such joy. His giggles make my insides glow and my heart feel twice the size. He's the most beautiful thing I have ever seen. There's deep contentment somewhere, but I'm still caught in a storm.

How am I?

Unsure.

Shell-shocked.

Overwhelmed but aware of my privilege.

Grateful.

Satisfied.

Terrified.

Totally in love. Like at a cellular level.

Anxious.

Irrational.

Moody as hell.

Bored of my own bullshit.

Weirdly proud of my son's poos.

Neurotic.

Numb.

Humbled.

Hopeful.

Creating a life is bewildering and blissful. I am forever
changed.

(For starters, my nipples will NEVER be the same.)

I'm just not myself.

But let's not talk about it. I don't have the energy.

It's hard, but we'll get there.

Let's just admire my delicious angel child.

You can have another hold.

Maybe you could hug me too.

I'm fine, honestly. Just tired

My girls, by Hayley Gardner

Shortlisted entry

-

My girls,

I am laid in bed and thinking about dying.

This has become ever so common for me.

Ever since those first 2 lines showed up on the discounted pregnancy test I bought from Amazon (because I refused to spend over £10 AND delivery on top of that)

This was back when Amazon prime didn't even exist and you had to wait 2 whole days for things to be delivered and to find things out, like "am I going to be having a baby?" and later "how do I stop my brain from thinking I'm going to die" which interestingly there aren't a lot of books on. They're all called reassuring things like "Think Yourself Happy" which is really fucking hard when all I could think about was all the terrifying things that could take you away from me.

I think that's a good thing to mention here, it was the fear of you being taken away from me that first made me lose my mind. I don't want you to feel guilt for that, it's just that's kind of what my love for you did. It made me insane with fear.

I couldn't even look at a door handle anymore, they were far too sharp to walk past with your wide open skull. Can you imagine that, being afraid of a door handle? Doesn't that sound ridiculous! But I'll bet if you ask your friends' mums at least one of them knows what it's like to be afraid of a door handle. Awful things.

When I started to lose my mind some of the first advice I was given was to speak with other mums. As though other mums would understand a woman that has stood barefoot in a garden at 11pm searching for magpies because she only saw one and one magpie meant you died in your sleep that night.

You see, the thing with magpies is that no one ever tells you the t&c's in relation to the rhyme. One for sorrow, two for joy…but can you see the same one twice or do they have to be together? What's the allowed time frame between seeing the first and the second? Who am I supposed to direct these questions to? Your life depended on it and no one seemed to care or have any answers.

I would find out later that, actually, loads of people understand that. Just no one dared talk about it with each other.

So I would sit in the garden.
And wait.

And then later, lie to my therapist about how I definitely didn't feel the need to do that anymore, whilst looking out of the hospital window and trying to disguise a salute as a head scratch as he asked me to rate my anxiety on a scale of how many days I was experiencing it. I lied again. I was bored of the sessions and there are so many magpies hanging out around hospitals that it's an absolute nightmare especially when no one will tell you the stipulations.

During the night I would call my health visitor and leave lengthy voicemails on her phone about how I was adamant you had caught a tropical disease. I would wake up in the morning ashamed, dreading her hearing the messages and fearing her returning my call. This happened multiple times until one day instead of returning my call she came to my house with a form that would diagnose me with PTSD.

It's amazing, really, to think that creating anything can be a traumatic experience. I never felt trauma as I carved my ducks out of clay as a child, or spread paint across a canvas as an adult. I didn't feel proud either. I just felt something that wasn't unpleasant. Something sort of calming. But now here I was having created the most incredible biological wonder of my life and a piece of paper told me it had been a trauma for me. My first experience ever of a creation that didn't calm me. I was handed the paper, awaited a phone call and just kind of felt sad and embarrassed that I didn't get motherhood right first try.

As you grew up and I had the space in my head to think about women creating life and the responsibility of doing so, I would laugh and think "of course this is traumatic, to call it anything less would diminish the sheer strength of those that endure it." I felt sad that I had ever doubted my ability to be your mum. Going insane for your children is absolutely natural and I would go on to completely lose myself in all three of you, each in very different ways.

And it's this losing myself in each of you that makes me think so often about dying. How now I simply cannot die, I cannot leave you behind in the world I pulled you into, I cannot be expected to not be there when you have feelings to discuss, I must now live forever to make sure you are safe in all that you do and be certain that losing my mind for you was the best thing I ever lost.

So I think about dying a lot as I drift off to sleep and secretly hope that your bodies still need mine should you wake in the night and that as we age together someone somewhere is busy working on a way to make this last for all eternity.

Forever your body in the night,
Mummy.

The Search, by Kirsty Crawford

Content guidance*: postpartum anxiety and depression, postpartum insomnia.*

-

Two of us left and three came back. Under the dark midnight ink of a January sky.

We jostled in through the door, wild with anticipation and the cluelessness of it all.

Immediately I missed the hospital ward. Tiny peas and mashed potato with a gooey crust. The comfort of the big orange button glowing faintly through the night, where, with one press, the answers would always come. *Yes, your baby will be sick quite a lot, he's clearing the fluid from his lungs. Yes, your iron levels are improving, we won't be sending you for a transfusion. Yes, we can remove the catheter after twelve hours and you won't feel it. No, you can't stay here.*

I missed the presence of the other newly minted mothers behind partitioned curtains. I missed them shifting in their sleep, their babies dozing beside in plastic cribs. I missed the quiet connection built by forging through the flames together on the same day.

Now I walk the house. Stained with milk and sweat and blood.

I look under things, picking them up, putting them down. I look in the fridge and above the cooker hood. I forget the names of things. I forget that my life used to have a running order and a rhythm, instead roaming the confinements of a house I don't recognise in the short spaces when the baby isn't at my breast.

When he is, we suffer and push and pull, my nipples cracked raw. The visiting midwives arrange us in a variety of poses like a Renaissance scene gone wrong. My husband takes photos of these, and I try bitterly to recreate the exact positioning, the baby protesting in hunger, his slippery mouth latching on and off and on and off.

Foreign objects cover familiar surfaces. A box of blood-thinning injections to be taken for ten days postpartum, silver nipple shields, liquid vitamin D drops, disposable gauze underwear, scratch mittens, cellular blankets.

Left behind are lonely, empty things that emphasise the size of the change that has swept over my life. A favourite candle half-burned, a book by the bed, an opened packet of pregnancy-craving cola bottles, a yoga mat hastily rolled away, used last to complete a sequence to spontaneously induce labour.

The sequence did not work.

I look at the house plants – thirsty and crispy. I try to feed the baby, feed the dog, feed myself, feed the plants. Sometimes I look at the TV where bright quiz-show contestants smile with a depth of emotion I can't recognise. I turn up the volume over the cries of the baby and hear nothing but the pulsing in my ears.

I am fizzing with raging cortisol and in complete sensory shutdown. I can't sleep. I'm scared of the dark. I wear earplugs in the day. Protein, sugars, and fat are taken from my bloodstream, making milk to give away more than ten times a day, but I cannot eat. The anxiety dissolves into deep heavy marshland and all I want is nothing. To do nothing and say nothing and be nothing. Postpartum insomnia, the greatest of all curses. Nobody warned me about this. How it feels to boil with frustration and watch a silent, sleeping baby as the night passes by and sleep skirts around my edges. In these black hallucinogenic moments, I am bereft, but I can also feel my new captor stealing my heart completely.

The daylight hours are short, and I am encouraged to walk outside in the winter sun. Reminded to drink water, take supplements and not compare the before and after. Motherhood is meant to change you they say earnestly.

I return from the outdoors with the pram and keep my feet moving, wearing a trodden path through the rooms in my house, still searching, still looking.

One day I stop mid-wander and look to the end of the hall. I look through the glass of the front door to a cherry tree outside. I look and I can see the ghost of my past leaving, squeezing an overdue bump inside a green duffle coat and swaying out through the narrow porch. I realise that she is who I've been hunting for. I want her to turn around and see the future looking back and at the same time I want another version of me, six months ahead, standing at the top of the stairs. I want one in the kitchen making cakes with a toddler, another in the garden on the first day of school. I want one on the sofa with a heartbroken teenager and one in the car ready to drive to her son's graduation. I want all the versions of me, all the possibilities, and I want them to stop and say, *'we promise it will all be okay'*.

I feel the chaos shift within me, and I know that this is the process.

The other side will be transcendent. The release of pressure will come, and one day the leech that clings and swells in my brain will slink off to forgotten shadows. The light will come through.

I know all this as I stare through the front door and mourn for that person I was, right on the cusp, when two left and three came back.

Uninvited, by Rachel Boyd

You wake to the sound of your stomach gurgling and wonder when you last ate. You check your watch, it's 10:45. You fight with yourself whether to get up or to try and sleep a little more but your stomach wins, as it often does. You tip toe from the living room where both Noah and Ellie are napping and put bread in the toaster and pour the sweet elixir of life: coffee. As the toast pops up so does a tiny voice below you, mine! he says, with his small hand, held out for the toasted soda. You lose, handing it over to him knowing you might get the soggy leftovers soon. The doorbell rings, the pitch wakes Ellie. She screams bloody murder which in turn activates Noah's tantrum. It takes everything in you to hold your own back. You see a blurry figure in the pane of glass in your front door, standing in blue uniform. *Fuck,* you think. How has it been another six weeks. You rush to let them in. Hi, you say opening the door, sweeping your hair up and away. Hello, she says, not

52

even looking at you. Making her way into your home, uninvited.

You lead her to the front room where Ellie squeals and Noah is on the floor with your toast smashed into the ground by a dinosaur. You're embarrassed, by the mess, the lingering smell and the TV as it plays some colourful trash disguised as education. You offer the woman some tea, she accepts and you're thankful for a moment to yourself. You leave kicking as many toys as you can out with you, making sure to close the door behind you this time. You have two minutes for the kettle to boil on the stove. You carefully kick your pyjama bottoms off and lift a pair of leggings out of the pile of clothes on your dining table. As the tea brews you reach for your secret cupboard. You take a chocolate digestive and you enjoy every single, blissful bite to yourself. You make sure no evidence is left and return with two cups of tea.

Noah babbles away as he thumps random keys on your piano. His buttery fingers all over your keys, it breaks your heart a little bit. The dust fills the room with each thud. You watch this woman sitting with such comfort on your sofa, with your newborn. You envy how effortless she makes it look as you set the tea down.

Poo, poo. Poo! Noah sings in tenor with the piano. Ahh sorry, he's learning the potty at the moment, you explain. She smiles and pauses, inspecting the mug of tea and sets it back down. Do you play? She motions her head to Noah, defiling your Piano.

You purse your lips. Rain starts to patter on the window. Not as much anymore, you say quietly.

So tell me how are you doing, she says.

I'm fine, you smile to really sell it.

How are you doing with sleep? she asks. You pull the sleeves of your top protectively round your wrists. Fine. I mean very little but fine, you smile again, not too much this time though, you can feel your dry lip is about to split.

Have you tried sleeping when she does? You pause for a second, Ellie fast asleep in this stranger's lap. Your son has lost interest in the piano now and kicks over a block tower with a boom that makes you jump. I'm trying my best with that, you say.

Do you want her back? she smiles at you, like she knows. Ellie is squirming on her lap and she lifts her to you. You imagine fleeing. You take Ellie off her and try to look comfortable with her in your arms. She lifts her notebook and takes a sip of the tea. She looks like she's trying not to spit it back into the mug, and you wonder was it definitely sugar you lifted? So, she says, we gave you the clear to have s-e-x at your six week check up didn't we? You pick at the little bit of dry skin on your bottom lip. Yes, you say, we're just too tired to be doing anything that could result in creating a quartet of them. She pauses, observing you and says, do you feel a connection to her? Your mind goes blank. You feel a hot panic from the core of you flush into your cheeks. The patter of the rain is louder, like wet fingers prodding the glass. *Will she take my children away, if I'm honest?* You think carefully about your choice of words. Of course I do, you mumble. She takes a moment. A moment to find the right words too, you assume. Well, she says delicately, your daughter has been looking up at you for the last five minutes and you haven't once looked down at her. You look down at her, holding back the lump forming in your throat. She's right. You feel nothing.

There's an uncomfortable silence as the health visitor gathers her things. You have your hands full, don't be afraid to ask for help if you need it, she says. *From who?* you wonder. She looks at her watch, I'd best be

off, good to see you again. You walk her to the door,
clutching Ellie close because that's what good mothers
do. Look after yourself, she says, touching your hand.
She uses her handbag to cover her head as she runs out
to the car, puddles splashing under her feet. You stand
waving one, two, three times watching the car reverse.
You look longingly as she drives away, dodging the
neighbours bin on the road. You wonder does she have
children? Does her home smell of sour milk and poo?
Does she have one of those homes full with plants and
candles that aren't constantly in threat of being
smashed. *Is this her dream,* you wonder. A dream to
visit tiny babies everyday and judge their exhausted
mums? Or perhaps she has something gathering dust
in her home too.

Navigating Motherhood and My Career, by Lauren Raybould

Ever since the age of 16, I have worked - whether it was hospitality, journalism, care work, or running my own business, I'd always made sure I worked. It became my entire personality, even working full-time hours alongside studying at university. I was so focused on my career that when my mother and I took a break to Paris, she said to me after one too many wines, "It's okay if you never have kids, you know," despite knowing I was in a relationship for a while. I was taken aback, as one day I wanted to have both and I'd fight like hell to maintain my career and have a family.

Having been in the throes of motherhood for five months now, I look back to What Life Was Like Before, to realise that my career defined me. Working all hours, keeping myself afloat as a bartender, obsessing over establishing myself as a journalist and then as a social media manager. That was me. If I didn't answer my phone, it was for one of two reasons: I was sleeping (rarely) or I was working. I was so much of a workaholic that both of my parents had said to me, when I was part way through my pregnancy, that they didn't expect me to have a family or have children because I was so career focused.

Having reconnected with an old friend after COVID, romance blossoming, and moving into our first house together with our pets, we decided it was time *to try.* Lo and behold, we welcomed our son in December last year, and ever since then, my identity has twisted and turned so drastically I have whiplash.

I was no longer defined by my work and that scared the hell out of me. This was unchartered waters here. I'm a partner, a fur mum, a human mum, a 'me' - whatever the hell that is. I'm a milk machine (or so it feels like), a comfort, a safety net, a teacher to this baby that is so new to the world and trying to navigate life.

I fretted over how I'd ever return to work now that I had this gurgling, raspberry-blowing, dribbly baby who had become my whole world. Praying for an iota of flexibility with my employers, I spent half my maternity leave anxiously going over the same concerns again and again. It came to a head when I realised, as I negotiated my KIT days, that they wouldn't be as flexible as I'd hoped and so here was the biggest decision of my career to date.

Do I stop breastfeeding so I can return to work with 3 days in the office, or do I quit so I can continue to breastfeed and start my own business?

I did something that even I couldn't predict. I resigned.

Once that email was sent, the relief crashed over me like a tsunami. I knew that it was the right decision, even if I had my hands tied over it. So, here I am, setting up my own marketing business while I raise my son. Who knows where this will take me, and maybe one day I'll return to working for someone else, but maybe not. I guess I'll just have to wait and see.

Now I enter a new era of identity and I look forward to navigating motherhood and my career.

My Dear Baby Boy, by Mairead Rawal

My Dear Baby Boy,

There are a few things I'd like to ask you. But only in my head, because I'll never say them out loud.

I wanted to ask how the happiest part of my day is when you wake, yet also is when you fall asleep? Can you tell that I long for the moment you finally stop fighting sleep and succumb to that deep, peaceful slumber only babies know? Then I impatiently, anxiously, wait for you to wake again, to stretch out those chubby arms, shape those rosebud lips into a perfect O and call for me.

And why do I crave for you to need me and not need me in equal measure? I yearn for a few hours' break from the relentless cycle of eat, sleep, poop, repeat, and your constant need to be held. Yet I miss you to my very core when you're away from me and count the minutes until you're wrapped in these arms again. They're weary when I hold you, but empty without you. How can I simultaneously want you near me but long for space?

How can I silently plead for help with this mammoth task that is motherhood, yet politely but firmly refuse any and every offer? I pray someone will sense my desperation and offer a hand, but then I can't bring myself to accept it when it arrives. Even when I feel I've emptied my last reserves, scraped dry my well of resources and can do no more, I hear myself proudly saying 'No thanks, I'm fine.'

I fret when your dad takes you out so I can rest, and worry about how many layers you have on or if the sunshade on the buggy is properly angled. Mostly, I worry whether you'll wonder where I am and feel frightened that I'm not with you. So why do I feel disappointed, offended even, when he returns you safely to me and says, "He was absolutely fine; he didn't even notice you were gone"?

How can I revel in the miracle that this amazing body formed and grew you, yet mourn for my prenatal body—the pert boobs, perky bum, and flat stomach (well, maybe not flat but only ever so slightly rounded)? I sustained you within these living walls, transforming you from something that could fit through the eye of a needle into a solid eight-pounder. How wonderful, how full of wonder I am that my body could do that. But…there's always a but. The saggy folds of skin, the stretch marks snaking around my hips, the dark shadows beneath my eyes - I do not like those one little bit. Every dent, dimple, and crease was worth it, I know it was. A more than fair swap for what I received in return - you. Still, is it okay to feel sad as I tuck my favourite underwear to the back of the drawer, no longer fitting, no longer flattering?

And why sometimes, in the middle of the night when I'm feeding you (again), do I want with every fibre of my being to lean over to your sleeping father, all gentle snores and rhythmic breathing, and slap his face in pure anger and frustration that he gets to rest and I don't? How can I actively dislike him and not want to be near him, but desperately miss him at the same time? I crave his closeness, his attention, his love in a way I've never done before. You, and don't take this the wrong way my darling, have irrevocably changed our relationship, severing habits and rituals honed to perfection over years of practise. But you have also helped us to forge brand new ones and create our new normal. We are a rope of three strands now, our relationship intrinsically different but ultimately stronger.

And why is motherhood so lonely when I'm never actually alone? As cute as that adorable little face of yours is, I do see it an awful lot! I sit with other mums at baby groups, surrounded by noise and chatter but

I've never felt more excluded. Did I miss the memo on how to make mum friends? Some women just breeze in, start a conversation, and leave with a new phone number. How do they do it? I have my friends, my husband, my family. They're all lovely, really, they are, but they don't get it. How can I tell them that I'm not enjoying every single moment of this role I desperately wanted and planned for? It's a lonely secret to guard.

And now, please don't be offended when I tell you this, but sometimes I don't really like you. Am I a bad person for saying that? There are moments, when I've microwaved my half-drunk cup of tea for the third time, and sour-smelling baby spit-up has crusted onto my top because I haven't managed to change it before it dried in, and you won't stop crying and go to sleep, and I don't like you. So how, even in those moments, on the very worst days, do I love you more than anyone or anything in my life? How is that possible?

But know this. Despite all I've said, because of all I've said, my life didn't truly begin until the day I first held you in my arms. I was simply waiting for you. And there is no bigger love in my heart than the love I hold for you, my precious, perfect little boy. It is an honour to be your mother.

Your Mama

P.S. Please go to sleep.

Burn, baby, burn, by Corinne Atherton

2012. For most, it was the year the Olympics came to the UK. For me, it was the beginning, but also, the end. The beginning of a love so intense, yet so exhausting. And the end of me as an individual.

We'd managed to leave the house at 8am that day. Quite an undertaking almost as impressive as competing in the Games when your first baby is only eight weeks old.

We stood at the side of the road; the crowd swarmed around us. I held my baby up so he could witness an athlete running past holding aloft the Olympic torch, its flame encased in its protective sconce. It was an event I hoped I could tell him about when he was older – a little memory of something exciting we did when he was tiny. I can't remember what we did for the rest of the day, but I was proud for getting out so early, proud for achieving that small thing.

Because at that time it could only be about the small wins.

I too had a burning flame of desire inside me, my body wrapped around it protectively. It was my will, my longing to do more, to become more than I had become. But my light was diminishing, rendered small, insignificant. All my time and energy was spent on my baby and his needs.

I would tell you I was tired, that was all. Tiredness was less loaded, less dangerous to admit to than the raging exasperation I felt. Tiredness could be cured. My burning frustration could not.

I was never ungrateful for my life with my new baby, I just longed for that time before. The time when I could do whatever I wanted, go wherever I wanted, with no proper responsibilities, no cares. It was the fist-clenching frustration at always having someone else on your mind, always having to consider someone else's life first. I was no longer the priority.

I couldn't simply pop out the door or go on a last-minute night out. I couldn't even go to a shop without a nappy bag, packed to overflowing with everything a baby could ever need, just in case.

That time was so hard – my flame almost went out. My little fire was constantly threatened by the water of my child's tears, his wetted little cheeks, a tiny body cool after a sweaty day of holding him close. Him suffering a cold, constantly teething, needing to be held, damp flesh against hot frustrated flesh. Ever-present, ever-comforting, ever-angry.

A mother's little helper allowed me to gain equilibrium. Hesitant conversations with close friends, new mums also, made me realise we all felt the same. But still it was taboo. We could never admit that our sparks were dimming, our flames guttering.

So, we told each other we were tired, that was all.

Yet still my little light kept burning. Deep down inside me it remained, although fragile, like a candle flame caught in a breeze. Stilted exchanges with other mothers who had proper jobs tormented me. They were able to let their lights shine brightly. I was a stay-at-home mum, what did I do all day?

The fire in my stomach burned for me to be more than just a mum. I still rebel against that now. That is not the sum of my parts. But am I allowed to feel what I feel: the desperate anxiety of trying to do everything, too aware of the knowledge that it's impossible, realising I can only do a half-arsed attempt at anything, in snatched moments of time?

Although with time, as the years pass, I gain clarity. The way I deal with it is to know that one day I will rise again. Tiredness will no longer be my default. I will require no excuse.

I will burn brightly with phosphorescent newness, having cast away my darkness, ready to be me once more.

So, I look ahead. I utilise fragments of time to plan, learn and dream. I will not pass through this phase unconsciously. I will live my season of motherhood quietly stoking that little fire, awaiting my moment to burst forth.

For now, I can use my glowing ember to warm my children's hearts and their home, keeping everything safe and cosy for them.

By 2040, when the Olympic Games is due to come to the UK again, my life will look vastly different to what it is presently. I will rise to the challenges I have set myself. My children, fully grown, will no longer need me like they do now.

I will look upon that Olympic flame and it will be diminished in the light of my own bright fire.

I won't say I'm tired.

I will be me again, that is all.

3:26am-3:26am, by Poppy Rowley

03:26am

Is it morning? Or night?

04:34am

Can't switch off. Headphones in, Netflix on. Episode
flows into episode.

05:15am

She is asleep and my eyelids are drooping

05:46am

She cries and I find myself clambering out from the
dark depths of deep sleep.

Groping at the edges, as I climb up

To settle

To calm

To be present

10:00am

Under the shower I rub my eyes

Trying to push away the tiredness

Push back into myself

Hoping heat will wash away

The steamy blur of my mind

Help me see clearly again

10:39am

"Breastfeeding is like running a marathon, you need
to fuel it" an Instagram post tells me and so I share a
snap of my second breakfast to my mum WhatsApp
group with the wild eyes, tongue out emoji

11:06am

Dashing down the hill for a mum and baby class, late.

They won't judge.

We're all in this together.

Right?

I manage to man handle...woman handle? Mother

handle? The oversized pram through the door

I gather bits and baby and join the circle

There's a candle.

We nod sagely at the shared trials and tribulations

"I got stuck bent over the cot, one tit hanging, trying

to feed him to sleep"

"He nearly fell off the bed"

"She did fall off the bed"

And

"Oh, she sat at 3 months"

"He's clapping...early"

"He's always slept through!"

"I really do love being a mum!"

12:46pm

As I walk home their voices pinball around my head

I look at other babies and I wonder if they sleep

through?

Two teenage boys, jostle along the pavement, and I wonder if they startle in their sleep, sit up in bed and cry

A group of men in high vis are sat on a wall, smoking and drinking cans of energy drink and I wonder if they thrash in the middle of the night crying out for their mum

Needing to be soothed and settled…

"You alright love? Need directions or something?"

I've been staring

I walk swiftly on

Glancing back, I see one twisting his finger at his temple, they all roar with laughter

It wasn't that long ago that I'd have got a wolf whistle from them, who'd have thought I'd miss that?

02:18pm

Sleep is like croissant crumbs, desperately collecting each one on the end of a licked fingertip, craving the

tiny morsels, not wanting a single flake to go to
waste.
She naps and my head falls back on the sofa, like I am
going under and it is delicious!

03:34pm
Maybe I could shave my legs, feel beautiful
Soft silky legs
A treat for me, and him.
In trying to forge a better world, I switched to a
reusable razor and blades,
Doing my bit.
I hold the metal. The glint of sun on the razor blade. It
is so...very...sharp...
I imagine the crimson pools
A beating glisten rising
I wonder what I would feel
To then feel nothing
No sound
No worry

No questions

No hammering thoughts

No cries

No guilt

No shame

And I press.

Gently oh so gently

….

04:46pm

We play hide and seek. Or maybe it's peek a boo?

Yes, it is, isn't it!

Need to remember to hang the washing out

What a big smile!

Haven't changed the bedsheets in weeks

Peek a boo!

That mug needs to go in the dishwasher

Can you do standing? Oh well done!

Need to unpack the dishwasher

Peek a boo!

Fuck what are we having for dinner?

05:05pm

Nappy change.

And it's me versus the alligator, a wrestling match

Her body contorts to escape the wet wipe

A foot slams down and stretches through the nappy

Poo between her toes and before I have time to grab

she kick-boxes me in the face and somehow manages

to wiggle her shitty piggies into my mouth.

08.31pm

My hand has gone numb from patting her bum

Trying to keep her asleep so I have enough time to

brush my teeth and wee and change into pyjamas

before she wakes again.

10:47pm

Check the monitor

Still asleep.

So we kiss deeply

Letting warmth melt

Leaning in

Inhaling

Feeling the soft

The hard

The tender

The touch

And then

We are broken apart by the green flash as the screen

lights up

She sits up

And cries

11:16pm

Curled around each other

A cinnamon swirl cuddle

My knees up, under her bum

Her legs softly nestled in my hip

She feeds

Letting off little grunt groans and nosey noises

Me reading

Eyes tired

The feeling of red rimmed

But desperate for this moment of creative absorption

00:37am

Little soft soft hand sneaks across my skin so gently.

Like a mosquito I want to bat it away but it keeps

coming back.

The sweetest irritation.

And I feel a scream rising

A banshee roar

Crawling and clutching up my throat

But no

No time for that now

Mustn't wake the baby mustn't wake the baby

02:26am

She. Will. Not. Settle. Doing night-time gymnastics.
One leg lifted high, rolling over and over and over and
she feeds and feeds and feeds and pulls away and
snuffles and cries out and feeds and pulls away and
cries out and feeds and snuffles and pulls away and
screams and tears flow and I must sleep but she. Will.
Not. Settle. And how can I complain when there is
genocide happening and atrocities in bedrooms round
the corner and pain and suffering and I am just a bit
frustrated…

02:32am
And just like that she sleeps. But I cannot
Thoughts are swirling
Maybe I'm not meant for this
Maybe I should have hysterectomied.
What would I have been
Where I might have been
Why did no one tell me this?

03:26am

She wakes.

I take a deep breath to steady myself, ready myself.

And then I look down at her and she beams

Her smile reaching from her soul to mine

Hooking me completely

And I would do anything

Everything

For her

Motherhood Unspoken, by Ellie Pulze

This is a collection of early motherhood poems sewn together by the thread of the unsaid.

When I became a mother, these were the things I wished I had permission to talk about, but often felt I couldn't. Fear of judgement or of seeming ungrateful kept me silent. After my second child was born, writing poetry helped me find my voice again. I hope these poems help you find yours.

Intrusions - A poem about intrusive thoughts

They tell you,

Long before their arrival,

How life will change.

Unrecognisable,

You'll transform;

The gentle letting go

Of all that was.

They don't tell you

Your mind will stray too.

The thoughts that shake and stir,

Blur your burnt-out edges.

Tears will come; hot weeping.

Fears will come; dark-night creeping,

Stealing through the cracks of you,

Drowning you in scum-water sweats

Of terror and dread.

Delusions and illusions

Born from a love so deep

You may sink.

That first time, unknowing,

Intrusions glowing shameful hot

Pressed away into lonely corners,

The 3am night-feed corners

Of my broken mind.

As I fall into the intrusions,

Fight or flight delusions,

The baby in my arms is calling, falling, falling.

Shame swallowed and spat out at 6am.

Reeling, heart racing, pacing

Another stretching day -

I pray, keep them at bay.

The thing no one tells you?

Your mind will stray.

Tested - A poem about the days that test you to your limits

You know this day,

The one that starts at 2.30am.

It cracks you open like their runny egg,

Leaves pieces of your shell on the floor

With the cheerios and soiled

Training pants.

Your yolk laid bare, dug out with sticky spoons and

grubby nails,

You leave trails of yourself across the worktops.

You'll piece yourself together with leftovers,

Lukewarm coffee, snatched cuddles

In the chaos.

It's the day no-one tells you about.

Your patience ran dry and your voice raised high.

You didn't cherish every moment.

You didn't feel blessed.

Just stretched thin and beaten, craving rest.

It tests you, presses you to the cracked

Mirror of motherhood,

Eyes wide with rage and fear and

Love like you never knew.

You'll survive this day.

You'll lay with little hands in yours,

A surrender that breaks and builds you.

You'll sink into the rest of another broken night.

And you'll show up again tomorrow.

I Choose You - A poem about the weight of the mental load

When it all seems to be too much
And Mama's head is bowed down low,
Know it's never bowed away from watching how you
shine and grow.
My little love, please know; it's never you, it's never
you,
It's all the other things that Mama has to be, and has
to do.

When life sometimes feels too heavy,
And Mama's shoulders sag and slump,
Know yours is a growing weight
That lifts me up in proud triumph.
My little love, please know; it's always you, it's always
you,
Who holds together my broken pieces with the
strongest kind of glue.

When sometimes Mama's empty cup

Cracks open with tired tears,

Know my open arms and hands

Still hold space for all your fears.

My little love, please know; I've space for you, I've space for you,

It's all the other things that Mama has to learn to say no to.

Of all the precious jobs that weigh upon a Mama's heart,

Know that loving you every day has been the easy part.

Over all the other things a Mama has to be and do,

My little love, please know; I choose you, I choose you.

Stitched Up – A poem about the "having it all" myth

We were raised strong girls

Them can rule the world girls

Break the glass ceiling girls

Snatch stars with glass-cut hands girls

You can have it all girls

Until those hands hold tiny pearls

Becoming tiny people's worlds

Do-it-all alone girls

Until your sanity unfurls

You are shattered glass left reeling

You become their starry ceiling

You enter this ward a full cup

You leave poured out, you leave stitched up

You Can't Catch Me – A poem about spinning all the plates

Run, run, as fast as you can,

You can't catch me, I'm a modern day mum.

I'm working like no-one else depends on me,

But mumming like my children are all that I see.

So follow my mantra, you too can have it all,

Listen up, move forward, and don't drop the ball.

Soak up every moment, enjoy every stage,

But don't let motherhood define you, break out of

that cage.

Feed on demand, but routine is key,

Put baby first, but take care of me.

Eat well, work out, prioritise sleep,

But keep baby beside you, keep the hours they keep.

Don't work 9 til 5, work flexi part-time,

Round 24/7 care-work that isn't paid a dime.

The early years are crucial, their brains wired for life,

So don't sweat the small stuff, and be a great wife.

Attachment, security, a safe base to call home;

Give them it all whilst you work from your phone.

My daily to-do list I'm powering through,

Dental check-ups, vaccines, a thousand photos of you.

No fussy eating, variety each day,

Fresh air in the morning keeps tantrums at bay.

Limit that screen time, and play them white noise;

The noise, all the noise, all the noise, all the noise.

I'm following my instinct and I read all the books,

I make decisions for everyone, and take care of my looks.

Her plates keep on spinning, this mum is the boss,

She keeps going, she runs faster, when she starts to feel lost.

The map is written for her, this modern day mum,

She doesn't need to slow down and turn her face to the sun.

Those little sunshines are the centre of her world,

But as she keeps going, her sanity unfurls.

This mum is on fire, she's powering through,

Her to-do list is crumbing, but isn't she too?

I Am Mother: The Invisible, by Emma Bacon

"I just feel invisible." My friend said to me one day early on in her motherhood experience.

"I just feel so utterly invisible. To everyone. To myself even."

Her second youngest child was screaming and crying in the background and her eldest, only slightly older child was shouting "Mummy." Over and over and over again.

My friend quietly sobbed, and I attempted to make soothing sounds down the phone whilst my own children ran around my feet screaming, arguing, begging me for snacks, for attention. Shouting for me, "Mummy" on endless repeat.

So, it seemed to everyone else we felt invisible, but to our children, we were very much visible.

It's been written about endlessly, talked about online, discussed on podcasts, shared amongst mothers at baby groups, you name it. That nothing quite fully prepares you for the moment your life, your physical body in fact splits into two. The fissure in time where you previously belonged to yourself and now wholly you are to give yourself to this little person that wants and needs you. And wants you so completely, that you swing from feeling so utterly overwhelmed, lonely and fearful amongst a wave of euphoric love.

Not only are you attempting to navigate a path not walked before, but you're bleeding heavily, leaking milk, crying, sweating, panicking. Working out how to hold the baby without dropping it, perhaps hobbling around with a catheter in. And no one. No one tells you this might happen beforehand.

I was convinced that I was going to breastfeed. Ever since I first imagined what being a mother might feel like, what I would be like as a mother. In my vision, I was breastfeeding and draped in loose cotton and I looked serene and beautiful. I was glowing and cuddling my baby.

Instead, I was almost a crash c-section, put under general anaesthetic after three failed spinal attempts and suspected sepsis. So, when I did wake up, I was surprised I had not died. And I barely remember my baby being brought to me, because as they passed her to me, I passed out again because I was so heavily drugged up.

And no one wanted to talk to me about this. No one.

"It's ok now Emma, baby is here safe and well. You are both here safe and well. That's all that matters.

That's all that matters.

It was like I was invisible to her. I was a ghost to myself. I do not remember so much of it. My first child. My first time having a baby.

And when I felt well enough to get out of the house, when I could finally walk after being sliced from hip to hip, and felt strong enough, no one looked at me. They looked at the baby in the pram. They wanted to know how the baby was. I not only looked like a ghost at giving birth, but I was remaining one. There was no celebration for my 36 hour labour, no daily soothing exercise to bring my body back to life, or support for my sense of self to step forward and return to me. I didn't know who I was anymore. And no one wanted to ask me either.

My friend said to me that day she phoned to tell me she felt invisible, the day she cried with exhaustion. She said, "Emma, did you ever notice women pushing pushchairs down the street before you had children? And I paused, and I thought about it, and then I said, "No, I don't think I did. They were 'just' mums."

"JUST" mums.

Because that's what they were at the time, before I had any vested interest in what being a mum or becoming a mum was like. In my ignorance, I was too busy worrying about where I was going to go out and who I was going to go out with.

My old, vacuous, empty life!

Little did I know that the most important people pounding the pavements night and day with loaded prams, were mothers. Were the women operating on two hours sleep if they were lucky, walking the same pavement routes around the block to help get their babies to sleep, or take their toddlers to the park. Plan meals, organise calendar dates, diary arrangements, school commitments, their own work dates. Keep up with friends and family, support their partners, attempt to look attractive still, when washing their body or faces would often come last because everyone else always comes first.

And yet we walk past mothers every day on the pavement, and they are invisible to us. Invisible to others.

How could they be? Why are they?

When I think of what my body endured. From conception, the months of growing said baby, to the point of going into labour, and how it nearly killed me both times, I look at my body with a pride so profound. And yet I feel nervous about the stretch marks, the changes, the bumps, the lumps, the extra weight. The fact I am getting older. That I am not young anymore. But look at how capable I was! Look at what my body as a mother made. An entirely brand new, never made before human being.

We should be celebrating it and singing it from the highest rooftops and amongst the streets. Women should be praised, they should be seen and heard as mothers. That they opened their bodies in sacrifice for their children and it should be seen as attractive, as something still sexy.

The term 'mother' is rarely used in the same sentence as 'sexy' and why not? Are we not women first and mothers second? We were considered so before we gave birth.

Mothers need to be visible. We need to not only "be" seen but "feel" seen. For there to be compassion, tenderness. Respect.

For we would be nothing, absolutely nothing, without our mothers.

Blossom and bees, by Lilly Allison

the things left unsaid are mainly the blossom

it overflows pink with bees

and you say 'more bee?'

and you want to see the fly up close and you smile at

the fly

and the cars, you say 'car car'

stroke the wheels

make your fingers black

these things are hard to say

they are like how the sun slants into a room

and so is the way you hurt me when you came into

the world

and then you were in my arms and I still cannot say

how much I love you

because it is too much

when you make that laugh I cannot say what it is

there is something in me that breaks

and I think it is the future

I have not said the 590 days of you

only the months of you

also, I cannot say your face

it is like a petal, it is like the ocean

how can I reason it?

there are many things unsaid

and the main thing left unsaid is the hurt

on that other side

mothers holding full warm shrouds

soaking the earth

while the blossom and the bees are there

and the sun

it is far far too much and cannot ever be said

or I think it would break the world

My Sad Nipples, by Debra Waters

Motherhood affects – or, perhaps more truthfully, afflicts – many parts of women's bodies. There's our heart, metaphorically speaking. And our head, of course, thanks to 'brain nausea', that constant parental worry we learn to live with. There's the stomach roil that accompanies said worry, and let us not forget our poor, beleaguered nethers.

Then there are nipples. Mine, I once thought with a hint of smugness, were meant for suckling. More bovine than human, there's never been anything dainty about them. Nipples the size of pinkie tips, areolae as big as side plates. I was born to breastfeed.

'It's fine to bottle-feed,' the midwife said. A happy mum means a happy child, she repeated, for the third time in our session. Nah, I've got this, I thought. I drank the odd glass of wine when I was pregnant; I'll take whatever drugs I need to get me through the birth; I won't be co-sleeping because I need space. But when it comes to breastfeeding, look at these puppies – they're made for it.

But there are things they don't tell you in NCT or birthing classes, things female relatives and other mothers don't share – things you wish your sisterhood had divulged. You wonder, even years later, why they didn't speak up, then you realise you didn't either.

Mothers carry hidden truths that weigh us down like stones in our pockets. These are a few that come to mind:

'I miss my pre-baby body'

'I don't enjoy playing with my kids'

'My life is not my own anymore'

'Parenting can be boring'.

One of mine is that when I nursed, the letdown let me down. Breastfeeding made me feel scared and homesick and angry and hateful and odd.

I find this out for myself, just like I discovered (during labour) that it can make you puke your guts up. Didn't read that in the books, didn't see that on the websites, didn't hear that from the midwives. I learned by vomiting mushroom ravioli all over the sofa, two contractions in. It felt like my last meal.

Then, a few days later, there came a realisation – I had sad nipples. It wasn't grief for what they once were – pert beacons of sexuality – but a repugnant response to the thing they are biologically meant to do.

Do animals get this, I wondered, when it happened – which was not immediately, but once the post-birth hormones and meds wore off. What about cats or wolves who have multiple suckled simultaneously?

How does this bizarre sense of agitation not send them mad?

I remember holding my baby in my arms; my little one, my bairn. For the first five minutes after he latched on, as my body sustained him, I told him how much I loved him over and over like a mantra until this inexplicable mess of feelings – of ire and ick – subsided and I could stroke his downy head without wanting to scream 'get off!'

There is a medical term for it, thankfully (can you imagine health professionals noting that 'Mrs X has a severe case of sad nipples', maybe even drawing a sad face emoji in the margin of an NHS notepad to clarify the point). It's called 'dysphoric milk ejection reflex', or 'D-MER' for short. Up to 9% of women can experience its effects. It's linked to a sudden decrease in dopamine – the same pleasure-cruising neurotransmitter that has us addicted to our phones.

It's also been around since time immemorial, yet studies are only a few decades old (no surprises there, given that women are the secondary sex in medical research). I assumed it was a symptom of postnatal depression, or an aversion to breastfeeding, but it's neither. It's physiological, not psychological. It's untreatable.

I stopped breastfeeding when my child was five-and-a-half months old. I expressed a while longer and guilt-pureed vegetables with the abandon of a mad scientist. I felt remorse while espousing that what was best for mum was best for baby. I never told anyone why I stopped, yet when it came to the squeamish details of childbirth I was all mouth. I still don't know why I didn't talk about it, or ever have. Every time I fed my child, I recognised that it would pass, so I endured it knowing that once I'd travelled through that chasm of discomfort I'd relax and connect with my baby. But an insidious melancholy coloured each feed and I came to dread them. It still makes me shudder.

My nipples are sad for other reasons now. They are sad that they will never breastfeed again, and they are sad that I'm ashamed of them. I should show them more kindness, sunbathe topless in the garden, perhaps, and let them bask in the warmth and light.

The Weight of Absence

Reflections on fertility, loss and grief

Birthday Party, by Chloe Lazenby

Shortlisted entry

Content guidance*: baby loss.*

–

Dear Rafe,

We went to the beach today - a perfect day for a celebration. The sun cut through the clouds and painted shadows, dappling the light across our faces as we drove towards the sea. The car was packed up with too many snacks and not enough towels. As we pulled away from the house, your sister bit into a ripe strawberry and juice dripped onto her dress. She stuck her sticky hands through the head rest, wiped the residue onto my hair and we all laughed.

She shouted with delight when she saw the sea through the windscreen and we parked on the hill overlooking the bay. The tide was low, the sea far away bargaining with the sand for space. We clattered down, setting up blankets and chairs as the party started to arrive. We held each other whilst cups of tea and coffee, steaming from flasks, were lifted up to the sky. Bellies warmed, we ran into the sea, splashing, gulping and diving into the murky shallows. Even though it is August, it is so cold it stings. I swam away from the crowd and paused for a moment of stillness. The seaweed circled my legs pulling me back and your sister put her arms around my neck. We pretended we were sea monsters, our salty limbs entwined like tentacles. She wanted to go on a quest to find you so we dove down and searched the sandy seafloor but you weren't there.

After our swim, we retreated to our camp and the picnic began to unfold. There were sandwiches stuffed with fillings, pastries stuffed with cheese, brightly coloured platters of vegetables and fruit. A proper party. Your auntie made a birthday cake, like she does every year, but as she was cutting generous slices and passing them round, a spirited dog came crashing into our picnic. It's wet, pink nose burrowing into the plates and sniffing out its chosen bounty.

Full of apologies, the dog walker grabbed the salty spaniel and asked your sister if it was her birthday. She looked up at him laughing the way children do when an adult makes a mistake, 'No, it's my brother's,' and as she answered, his eyes fell to your name etched into the sand and he caught my eye as I felt my neck for your locket. Everybody looked at your name, gently reminded that it was your birthday but you are not here. This celebration is for you and about you but you are missing. You can't ask to blow your candles out over and over again, or race your cousins down to the sea.

When we were last together, I tried to say it all. Hastily and in whispers pressed against your little ear, I told you the things that you needed to know but I missed out so much. The mundanity of conversation, the quips, sayings, absent minded love yous or hurry ups are all left unsaid. You heard us name you on the day you were born but you will never say your own name.

I wish I could ask you to put your shoes on or to give me a hug. I wish we could say things to each other that we forget because they are boring and insignificant. I wish we had had more than those hushed, precious words.

Mummy x

Friendships and fertility, by Laura Hughes-Onslow

Content guidance: *pregnancy loss and fertility struggles.*

-

To my best friend,

I always thought you'd be the first one to have a baby.

You're the eldest of four, and you have maternal energy that I've always admired. You can steady a wriggling baby in your arms, cooing whilst holding conversation with the mother. You teach little ones. You taught me about basal body temperature and egg-white discharge and folic acid. You were with a partner for eight years, and he went back and forth on having children, and I saw how it tortured you, until things ended, and you met someone who was sure from the beginning. We checked.

You got married last year and went on honeymoon. He joked about the hardships of trying. From Italy, you sent a photo of your wide smiles under straw hats. Behind you there was a sign: 'Via Dell Amore'.

I got a call from you late on a Wednesday – unheard of on a school night – and I squealed with delight and laughed as you shared your news. A honeymoon conception, how perfect. You were the first person I told, a full circle moment.

When my baby was born, I wrote endlessly, tapping into phone notes to clear my overwhelm. My poems had long since dried up with my milk, but over a hot coffee, the words flowed:

<u>Fertile Ground</u>

Woke up with a smile
Remembering your news last night
I know we hold this lightly now
Weeks and weeks of fruit seeds
You held my hopes with me

The truest hearts

Took a stroll down love street,

Together

What did you expect -

It was fertile ground

Crystals under pillows

Edging into dreams

Questioning the cards

Is it all as it seems

I don't know if there's a plan

My dear friend

But it feels like fertile ground

And I don't know if I believe

in a plan,

But it feels like we are walking

On Fertile Ground

You said 'wow - it feels magic, like a spell'.

I was imagining our children playing together, I planned to send you books and articles I'd found helpful.

And then, a few weeks later, you messaged me. 'I've had a bit of bleeding'.

SHIT.

I felt sick. And really embarrassed about the poem.

The lessons then came thick and fast and were truly devastating. You taught me about what normal rising levels of HCG should look like, and what a subchorionic haematoma means. And you taught me how five months later your best friend still might not be quite herself after a miscarriage. You were quieter, more solemn, for a while.

I stopped sending you pictures of his face covered in spaghetti sauce. You sent me a single blood drop emoji when your period started, and I sent you a heart back, every time.

I don't think we talk enough, maybe at all, about how fertility and parenthood can affect our friendships.

It's so fucking hard.

I have a lullaby for my baby - the sea goes in, the sea goes out - it's got the right cadence to send him to sleep, and it calms me also.

We are standing on the beach, and the sand is constantly shifting beneath our feet.

Is there a way of standing firm? Can we face each other authentically, sensitively, with open hearts, to avoid being washed to and fro. She's one of the strongest people I've ever met. If there's a way, she will show me.

Another one of my best friends has just found out she's pregnant after eight months of trying. She was just about to start IVF. Sounds simple when it's reduced to two sentences, but it's been a huge mental ordeal for her. Shifting sands, constantly.

Have I learnt my lesson?

I share a poem with her:

Two Blue

I've been holding hope

Alongside you

Waking up to a message

Of two blue

Blew me away

It's a first step

I say

We aren't getting excited yet

You say

But I can't help how I feel

And it's peace, and it's joy, and it's potential

You're exhausted and can't drink coffee

You're having weird dreams

You're emotional

And you're not an emotional person

Usually

You take things in your stride

And this is a big first step

I'll match your pace

I'm here beside you

I'll carry your hope and excitement

We can look at it when you're ready

Two blue

I love you

She cries and say, 'Omg that got me going'. We blame the hormones.

The sea goes in, the sea goes out. We stand on the shore, and we hope. 490 more times, thereabouts.

Maybe next lifetime, by Precious McCarthy

Content guidance*: fertility treatment, childlessness, mental health, thoughts of self-harm, racial inequality.*

-

Let's start where all good stories do, in the communal area of the ladies' - this time at a former friend's hen do. Naturally it involved copious amounts of alcohol and said friend needing to be helped to the toilet, so down we went.

As I came out of my toilet cubicle, without warning the word vomit erupted. She began to rant at me, telling me how unfair it was that she was being made to wait before she could start IVF. She knew she wanted to have a child and given the circumstances why did she have to wait? How unfair it was that there were people with 'healthy wombs' who didn't want to have kids.

"How can you not want to have a child?" she said, shouting her question at me and the world.

The bride-to-be was already going through a challenging few months with a death in the family, and a recent diagnosis confirming that conceiving and carrying a child would be difficult. So I decided to give her a pass. My mind told my mouth not to engage with the entitled and nasty comments she spewed at me and we returned upstairs. I've thought about that conversation on and off ever since; regretting not responding with how I truly felt on the matter.

Growing up I'd never envisioned marriage for myself. Out of the women in my immediate family, only my gran has ever been married. I saw my mum and aunt raising children successfully without having to be someone's wife. And so the idea has always felt antiquated and alien to me. What did feel familiar was the idea of having children and up until my late 20s, it was a given.

And then I started to question it all. Did I want children because it was expected of me? Because that's just what you did? Meet someone, fall in love, get married, buy a house and have children - all in that order. For the last 3 or 4 years I've been interrogating if having a child is really what I want.

To start, there's the lack of sleep, freedom and the constant worrying. There's also the cost of raising a child in the UK until they reach 18 - on average around £166,000 for couples and £220,000 for single parents (*Child Poverty Action Group 'the cost of a child' report, 2023*). And to be honest, these figures aren't an accurate reflection of the times, with people living with parents well into their 20s due to the high cost of living. Then there's the fact that as a Black woman I'm 4 times more likely to walk into a hospital pregnant and not come back out alive (*MBRRACE-UK 'Saving Lives, Improving Mothers' Care' report, 2023*). As well as the general state of the world and a kind of guilt attached to bringing a child into it. Especially bringing a mixed heritage child into the world, who will have to be confronted with why some people who look like their dad, treat people who look like their mum in the most horrendous ways.

That being said, with all of these considerations whirling around in my head, they're really just the tip of the iceberg. Because underneath it all, what does motherhood look like for someone with chronic depression? I've suffered from a depressive disorder for as long as I can remember, officially being diagnosed at the age of 21. For the last ten years I've been on and off antidepressants and had years of therapy. And while I'm in a much better place than where I was at 21, I'm still very much struggling.

I've not yet managed to break my pattern of suddenly stopping my medication (heavily advised against), often resulting in self-destructive behaviour along the lines of self-sabotaging my relationship and drinking more than usual. There's also a type of tiredness, sadness, brain fog, emotional coldness and rage that feels indescribable. Showing up as a constant urge to stay in bed all day unshowered, thoughts of helplessness, low self-esteem, nasty comments in my head and out loud and breakdowns over the smallest of things. I start to feel myself shutting down and I'm paralysed with the fear that my partner is going to leave me. That's even without going into how my inherited eating disorder and body dysmorphia both become even more ferocious during this period. These are all things I've discussed in hours of therapy, yet I still can't seem to shake.

On my meds, all of the above still apply. But the breakdowns become less frequent, the negative thoughts not so loud, the self-destructive behaviour appears less and so on. But it's still there, waiting to be triggered by something or for me to fall off the wagon and stop taking my meds again. For me, when I think about adding a small human to the mix, it sounds like a recipe for disaster. The pressure I know I would put on myself to try and do it all while feeling like I want to walk in front of a bus. Not to mention the pressure on my partner.

That's not to say that I don't wonder sometimes what our child would look like and who they would grow up to be. Pushing my belly out just to pretend for a moment. But then I look in the mirror. And I'm quickly snapped back to reality when that wonder is overshadowed by the deep and complex feelings about gaining weight and my body changing. Who knows, maybe one day soon I will feel well enough to consider having a baby. Or maybe that one day will have to wait another lifetime.

After Dad, by Jacqui Crowley

Content guidance: losing a partner.

-

I have felt like half a parent sometimes, not just Mum, the responsibility for all of it with no one to talk it through. I have no understanding of these people that say you have to be Mum and Dad. I don't know what it is to be a Dad. I know what it is to grow human beings within myself and be the source of nutrition for a helpless person. Physically connected to the growing and knowing this new person but trying to share it with your Dad. I remember when you used to wake when I was pregnant and I would spoon your Dad and press my belly into his back so he could feel you kick.

My experience of becoming a mother was more physical than his experience of becoming a father. When you were newborn, a lot more of it was our personalities and strengths that defined our roles. He would stay up with you while I got some sleep and then bring you up for a feed. It's not like he was good at DIY or barbeques or sport. But that's just hobbies, not the definition of a Dad. Equally, being a mother wasn't just about me staying home and coordinating all your activities. Won't deny that I still do that - and I did wish he could be able to switch as quickly to the new routines.

You've been great kids. Oh yes, I have been frustrated with your stubbornness and unwillingness to do stuff. That's individuals for you. With everything that went on, I can look back and think at least feelings have been out in the open. You haven't pushed them all down and ignored them to spare my feelings, or anyone else's. Your dark sense of humour may surprise some but I find it funny.

At times, the guilt of being the parent left, has been overwhelming. We were a team, your Dad and me. I am grateful for you being part of your Dad's legacy as well as mine. Motherhood was so much easier with him here - having that second adult with our family's best interest in mind - not just for planning the future but for fun stuff. He was good with holidays. He was great at travel, long distance driving as well as the admin.

I have spent years terrified of doing something in case I leave you without either parent. I don't like to leave you for any length of time. I don't like to go on long drives without you. I have seen you lose one parent, and I can't bear the thought of you losing another. It's amazing I still drive to be honest.

I am sorry I couldn't take on the 'live life to the full' attitude in the early days. I am sorry that for so long I was so numb with grief. Even now I feel guilty when you hug me because we've been watching some film or drama that uses death of a parent as a plot driver because you've seen me cry.

I am glad that your Dad wasn't just a glorified babysitter. He facilitated me being able to follow my interests and hobbies. Even being support crew for events, with you in tow. And that has been an important part of being able to carry on being your Mum in the difficult times. I have had to have something for me, particularly something physical to keep me well so I can carry on supporting you. It's that 'please ensure you put on your oxygen mask before assisting someone else' scenario. You have to be well enough to keep going. There were times when I raged about the expectations of others and I would be telling them that if I fall apart it all falls apart.

I did my best. And I like to think that in most instances it was much better than the worst. In the early days, I could only do what needed to be done. Without you,

I'm not sure I would have done anything. Nothing compares to the helplessness when you cried wanting your Dad back.

Now motherhood is less physical and hands on. It's been a learning process for me to balance you developing independence and me not being fully in control. Trying to give you the space to grow without me. And then the times when you still want me to walk you through something. It would be nice if you listened to some of the suggestions first time round, but given I'm your mother it's hardly surprising you won't take advice, or check some important detail.

With any luck, good fortune and improvements in health, I will have many more years of motherhood. I hope that I don't leave things unsaid about how proud I am of you. Although you could do a bit more around the house.

Pathological Mother, by Ruth Stevenson

Content guidance: *baby loss.*

-

There was a bear in the zoo

That ate two of her babies.

The zookeepers couldn't understand.

How *could* she?

Why would she?

Perhaps they were sick.

Perhaps *she* is sick.

In the wild it happens too

If a mother cannot feed her young

If one of her babies dies

She will eat it

It will nourish her

It will save the others,

Sometimes.

Or maybe it's just pathological behaviour

They say.

But no one knows for sure

They say.

I do.

I understand.

When I saw your tiny body

Curled in a kidney tin

That matched the curve of your too pale limbs

I understood.

The urge to pop you in my mouth

Was overwhelming.

I wanted to reabsorb you

Put you back where you belonged.

Part of me.

But I didn't.

I never told anyone.

I didn't want to be called pathological

Knew no one else would understand.

Except those others

Those mothers

In their wilderness.

The parts that I left out, by Carina Wan

Content guidance*: cancer, death and infertility.*

-

Six years have passed since you've been gone. I promised myself that I would write to you each year to keep you updated, but life got in the way.

It would have been your 40th this year and I often wonder whether you would have been a mother too by now. That had always been your plan. When you got your diagnosis and then the relentless disappointments that followed, the likelihood of infertility had been the knife twist.

You had been heartbroken, so angry at the thought of having that opportunity taken away from you. As if it wasn't enough to have to live with the fear of losing your own life, but you had to keep going with the knowledge that you wouldn't be able to create a life either.

When I first found out that I was pregnant I was scared to tell you. I knew you resented me for surviving my cancer (you had said so yourself), and now this. A pregnancy out of the blue, when they had all but told me that it wasn't going to happen. But I needn't have worried. You were over the moon for me. You said it gave you hope that one day you might be able to be a mum after all.

I'm sorry that never happened.

I look back now at all the things you did which were like acts of a mother-in-waiting. The homemade Christmas decorations that your housemate still hangs each year, the cellophane wrapped shortbreads you lovingly tied with ribbon before presenting to each of your friends, the lopsided gingerbread house that we built together that I had to carry on my lap in that taxi, terrified that the next speed bump would be the end of it.

So, I thought maybe for my first letter to you, I could tell you a bit about what it's like to become a mother, to grow a person. I know it doesn't compare to having your own, but I want to show you some of the unseen footage, to give you the director's cut.

I guess I should start by saying it's not how I thought it would be. Maybe everyone says that? But what I mean is that it's not possible to comprehend the totality of it all. Perhaps you can imagine the-surge of love that can stop your heart, or what it feels like to be so exhausted every conversation sounds like an echo. But nothing can prepare you for the fear that comes along too. No one told me that as soon as my babies were here, the deep love I felt for them would be matched, if not overshadowed, by the constant fear of losing them.

I live now, with an ever-palpable sense of foreboding. I have seen my children die a thousand deaths. Flung from my arms and dropped as newborns down a flight of stairs. Suffocated in the folds of my flesh because I fell asleep during a feed. From a head injury at the playground when I don't make it to the open side of the climbing frame in time. (Who designs these things?) I sometimes hear the scream that would erupt from me, silently inside my head.

I too have met all manner of grisly ends. Pushed onto a train track by a random stranger, leaving my family to wonder why I had done it; in tragic car accidents and panicked plane crashes, at the violent hands of a man who follows me home from the station, or from long, drawn our battles like your own. So persistent are these intrusive thoughts that I sometimes find myself coming to with a jolt, eyes wide, my heart in my throat.

You probably think I'm being dramatic, or making it seem worse than it is, to be kind. But I can't tell you about the light that floods my body whenever I feel their fingers wrap around mine, without showing you the dark that seeps into my mind whenever they are too still as they sleep.

Of course that's not all of it. There is so much beauty to be found too. But I feel like you know about that. That's the reason so many of us choose to be mums; so we may lay next to our children, breathing them in, running our fingers across their pillowy cheeks and watching their eyelashes flutter as they stare back at us. I'm sure I don't need to share the hazy slow-motion frames of their joyful faces as they run through water fountains, pick daisies in the park or call you mama for the first time. We know all that. We've been shown it a million times.

But no one explained what would happen to *me*, once I became a mother. No one told me that I might feel like a paper doll that's been ripped to pieces, and crudely stuck back together, misaligned, fragments still missing. I must have missed the memo that said my own voice would have to fight for space in my head, and I would struggle to hear her above the "mummy, mummy, mummy, look at this!"

It doesn't last forever. But it does linger. And I can't help but wonder whether I would have been a different, (better), mother had I known that I would have to relinquish parts of myself. Maybe people did try to tell me. I know that I have tried to prepare friends with raw honesty that probably sounded like ingratitude. And it didn't make the slightest bit of difference. For those who have gone on to have kids, they do now finally understand.

Were you still here, I imagine you'd put my words in storage too; bullishly place one foot after another into Motherhood regardless; heart open and soul willing to be turned inside out.

I wouldn't blame you. Even after all I've just shared, I'd probably do the same.

For Oliver's Mum, by Lisa Broom

The author of this poem worked in a women's refuge for several years, gaining insight into the lived realities of domestic violence. The mother and child depicted in this poem are entirely fictional and the author is writing under a pseudonym. In creating this piece, the author wove together elements from a variety of experiences, carefully fictionalising and generalising them to speak to a wider truth. No specific individual is portrayed.

Content guidance: themes of violence, domestic abuse, sexual assault and child loss.

-

It seems you have gone back

Re directed back on track

For bruises, and systematic crack

Of bone and heart

Despite what done, despite what said

You've returned to life of dread

Possibly already dead

Or come apart

I know, I know it was unfair,

That he who dragged you by the hair

Was free whilst you were stuck in here

It is outrageous!

But that is how the system is

They bailed him to the place you live

Effectively the place is his.

It's dangerous.

I know you missed the things you knew

Your family, friends, the place you grew

I realise how your anger stewed.

But to disappear!?

This is a safe, safe place

A house with cameras, no real face

Somewhere he would never trace

You were safe here

Now back?! - Despite all we tried

to reassure you as you cried

and told us how your foetus died

at his boot

How he raped you and then called you whore

Smashed your head against the door

Made you eat from off the floor

How he drunk

How he tore your baby from your breast

Told you how you had to dress

Beat you if you did protest

How low you sunk

How he put his fags out on the cat

Called you ugly, called you fat

How he shouted, how he spat

His threatening sneer

How he stole and sold your stuff

Randomly gave you a cuff.

How no was never good enough

How you lived in fear.

And your little boy? What of he?

After what he saw, now more must see?

After he felt safe and free?

Now back to that?

We'll pack your odds and sods, your clothes

I'll do the paper work. Your case will close

But I won't give up hope . Who Knows

You might make it back

An audience with my decisions, by Julia Kendal

Content guidance: pregnancy loss and infertility.

-

They've been sitting quietly, the decisions that accompanied me here. Patient, but weighted. They carry their consequences, but also the fact of having to be made at all, or unmade, or remade again and again... The stage has been cleared, a circle formed, so for once we can look each other in the eye. Besides, they've never been very good at straight lines. Not so much a path; more of a net. One that in turns seems to hold me off the uneven ground, trap me, feed me when my hand would falter. It's time for a little unravelling.

First up is the choice to try. It's a lot grubbier nine years on. Been turned over, again and again, by steady but bruised hands. It was never bubblegum bright to begin with; we started out with the knowledge, but not really the understanding, that this was not going to be easy. A set of limitations present since conception but misdiagnosed until aged 20. I used to be grateful not to live under the blanket 'no' it hands men; a 'maybe' seemed hopeful back then. So many hushed years later, it sits a little differently.

Then, the move to share from the start. Simple, if only because we glimpsed just enough to know we would need people. Over the years, they've carried hope, faith and tears for us, so we didn't have to find them alone. We meet each other in the middle of the floor like old friends.

Next, the decision not to try IVF again. I will always be glad we did a round, and smile at the lives it started, even if neither saw out the term. I'll never regret those two. But it still stands tall, the decision not to go again with the needles. And beside it, the closing of the door on adoption; a beautiful gift for so many, and one that

– for us – would be too much about our own life ambitions and nowhere near enough about the child in need of a home. Two pillars, polished and upright.

And yet, they muddy the story that surrounds us. To speak of decisions implies a mastery of language that I do not have. Identifying with neither 'childless' nor 'childfree'; I can't escape the fact of our babies' existence or live out parenting as a daily reality. 'Not by choice' has also begun to feel increasingly disingenuous. I did not choose the genetic condition that fractures our chances. But we have not been inactive in this journey. We wanted to have kids more than almost anything – and yet we did not to pursue it at any cost. So our focus became more about how to live this out well.

These are the choices that begin to crowd the floor.

Tiny ones, usually unseen, made of grit. The offer of a word of sympathy when someone says how hard it was to try for one year before getting pregnant. I make myself take this at face value, hold the space for the possibility that your twelve months could be more devastating for you than my hundred plus have been for me. That is how you felt; I will hear it.

Relentless ones, because being in our thirties means we are in the heat of this season. Fitting our lives to playtimes, mealtimes, bedtimes. I am glad that this is part of our friendship offering: to flex, to travel, to mould to a time and place that serves other families' lives. And at the same time, it's precious when one of you crosses our threshold. Or bends for our boundaries too.

Choosing peace has been copious decisions in the dark. And yet, sometimes, they barely feel like a choice at all. Because the alternative is unthinkable. Cut out, cut away. Isolated from relationships that have travelled decades. Alone in a town heaving with families. But more fundamentally, it would be to cut myself off from my own core. My own values. Ones that prize that a conversation can hold the contrasting tenor of your motherhood frustrations and mine. And the opposite joys; your daughter's violin lesson alongside my Saturday lie-in.

We take a moment for the empty seats. The moments fallen by the wayside, that I can't even honour with memory. They are probably part of how we got here too.

What is the point of this play?

I have been growing a little less easy in this story. Most of the time, we live in the good of the joy we are walking out. But the creeping thought has emerged in recent months: have we chosen our peace a little too well? Too present, too fine, for it to be questioned. Doubt emerges from the silences; the fading of messages checking in on key dates or particularly familial moments. Barely a chat about how we feel about it now. I suspect these thoughts lurk in minds but don't make it to lips or texts. Just occasionally, I wish they would.

I survey the stage, untidy with the crowd. They remind me that: I truly am ok. That our life is rich, not swamped by the grief that we've learned to live with pretty well. And that means, there are still days when I miss my children. The ones who didn't get to be born and the ones who never even existed. There are some moments when I could feel like the victim of our own success. But I nudge myself: don't despise the potential to thrive. Being here, in this house, in this town, in this world, with families who love you, and children who shout your name and lead you by the belt of your dress to meet their chickens, and friends who thank you for the meal you brought while you hold their snuffling second-born so they can finish feeding their first. This is the peace you've chosen. Let it tangle you in life again.

My Aaron, by Karen Constantine

Content guidance*: teen death.*

-

My Aaron,

my dear, my beloved boy, my lost one, and my favourite, (for God's sake, don't tell your siblings I said that!)

Please don't ask me why it's taken me more than your nineteen years on the planet to put pen to paper...

I've a great deal to write.

It's been nearly a quarter of a century; we need a catch up!

First a confession. I know now, I was selfish and stupid to have you in the first place. Hear me out please? I would have told you by now, would've explained, if only you'd been here to listen. If only you were within touching distance. If only I could feel the curve of you again, the weight of your muscled arm splayed across my shoulder, or the heat of your head, with its sunlit copper tones, as you stood – as you always did – against me, under my breasts, threatening, 'I'm gonna get as tall as you mumma!' And you did. And ha! I never expected you to grow. Too young at nineteen to anticipate baby-to-boy, boy-to-man. Unaware that time would race like a river in flood. That cells would multiply.

Aaron, I'd say to any mum now, 'Relish it all, don't miss a second, don't mind a moment, cherish every heartbeat.' I'd say the same to me – back then. I think deep down on a cellular level I knew it, but even so... we all need to be reminded.

Is there any way to tame time to treacle?

Or a potion to freeze and hold; your first tooth, your first steps, your first words, your first everything?

I guess you do know that the heart beats steady only until its end. That was something you taught me. It wasn't a fair trade, Aaron. I only taught you to brush your teeth, tie your laces, tell the time, do your homework, be back before nine, and call me. You always called me. Thank you.

I'm in my sixties now, I think you'd still recognise me – my eyes are the same, I'm wider, greyer, slower. We'd probably pick up just where we left off. 'Use condoms. Clean pants. Be careful. Take your coffee cups downstairs.'

Hey, do you remember the time I painted your bedroom jet black? Everyone thought I was mad. The crazy mother and her sunny son. Do you remember camping in France? Swimming in Skiathos? Your brother? Your sisters? They mourn you still, the years don't make grieving easier… our family jigsaw can never be complete. Not now.

Do you remember Bobby? He's got a family now. Loads of kids. I think they give him hell – just like he did to Bobby Snr. And remember Duff? He has the most adorable girl. And Emma? She's inventing implausible cocktails on the Costa Del Sol.

When I had you, nothing was right. We had a freezing house, could barely afford food. The marriage was as threadbare as everything else. Destined to fail. A sensible person might have waited – but I was compelled by all the heavenly stars, and along you came to join your brother. In any case, Aaron, I believed then, as I believe now, you *chose* me to be your mother. I'm certain you did. How lucky I was.

Just yesterday I read about how a bi-directional transfer of microchimeric cells, mother-to-baby and baby-to-mother occurs at birth. My heart soared up and light, in a way it hasn't all these long, sad years. The scientists say it doesn't mean anything, like a belly button, it serves no purpose. But now I know, with this hard proof, with this verified fact, as long as I'm alive, so are you. So. Are. You. You see, scientists don't know everything, they can't quantify love.

After all these years, when I've truly feared telling other mothers that you went before me, now, hand on my heart, I can say you live on. You are a physical part of me. You live in me.

That's what I can say to other mums.

At Least, by Jade Buss

Dear At least,

Can you write to a phrase? I hope so, I hope very much that you can see this and know the power you hold.

Two words that in an instant minimise experiences, the struggles, the challenges. Belittling the situation and silencing my voice.

I first heard you in my journey to motherhood at 10 years old. Standing in the sick room, blood on my frill trimmed white knickers. Hearing the rest of year 6 running past out to playtime. The receptionist dangling a key in front of me. Here you come. "At least you can use the special toilet now"

The special toilet, the mystery behind the locked door was now mine to discover. Instead of a sanitary bin and cushioned toilet paper, I would have liked an explanation of what was happening to me, why my tummy hurt.

You seem to be in place ready to go, to shut down conversations. To stop things getting awkward.

"At least you know you can get pregnant" A pat on the thigh and off to put the kettle on. I'm crippled over in agony, knowing my baby was slipping away from me, and not for the first time. You are there, a consolation prize in this horror.

Why are you the words we choose? Why not open the conversation up "I'm so sorry you have lost another baby, why don't you have a cry, tell me how you feel?"

Because it would make people feel uncomfortable. The less said about it the better.

You have been there at every point of my life as a mother. When I begin to share my struggles, you remind me that I should be thankful. My pain isn't really valid compared to greater suffering.

I get that you sometimes are intending to comfort, but you so often silence the complexities. Not allowing a rebuttal, but do I really need to? Should I just nod and agree?

"At least you can get some sleep while he's in special care"

Nod.

No of course I am not going to sleep, how could I even let my eyelids drop for a second more while my son is lying under a blue light, wires and tubes running over his body like veins. A piece of me torn away.

You come again.

"At least you didn't have to push her out"

Nod.

However 19 hours ago I was on a operating table, while they sliced through 7 layers of skin and muscles, then to spend the next few hours alone in a ward, with a screaming daughter who I couldn't reach because I was on a drip, catheter bag filling up, no one to help as they were obviously short staffed. But no, you're right, what a relief I didn't have to push.

"At least you have one of each"

Nod.

You make me feel ungrateful at times. When I found out that because of medical negligence I couldn't have any more children. The happy memories of all my siblings filling every inch of my childhood home with laughter and love were dreams that would not be mine. My family had been completed by the act of another.

Walking along with a gaggle of nieces and nephews at my ankles, babes in arms, you appear.

"At least you get to give them ones back"

Nod.

How I long to have one more hazy 2 am dream feed. The house still, a mess, but I've carved out a space on the bed. Dim lights, newborn smells, snuffling noises as I fill their belly, knowing that my body is fuelling theirs. Stroking their hair as time stands still.

I haven't learnt to fully see beyond you, nor have I embraced the entirety of my journey without your haunting presence. Each time I hear you, a part of me still aches, feeling unseen and misunderstood.

My story remains entangled with you, and I struggle to free my feelings from the weight of you.

Perhaps someday I will move beyond you but for now you linger, a shadow over my experiences. A testament to the things left unsaid.

To the baby I never met, by Cait Gwilym-Edwards

Content guidance*: grief, baby loss.*

-

To the baby I never met,

I'm sorry. This feels silly writing a letter to you when you will never read it. It makes you feel more real, being able to leave things for you. Even though we never met I hope you know how much you are loved. I am sorry you were denied the chance to experience all the best things life has to offer. I am sorry you never got to know how it feels to lie in my arms. I'm sorry you never got to hear your daddy's laugh. I'm sorry I never got to hear yours. I am sorry you didn't get to learn what fresh fallen rain smells like. I'm sorry your finger paintings will never cover every space on the fridge. I'm sorry you will never feel the sea breeze on your skin. I'm sorry you will never fall in love, or get married, or have a child of your own. I'm sorry that I failed you so much in those ways. I'm sorry that your life with me was taken. I am sorry that I could not do my job and protect you.

I wish I knew what colour eyes you have; your whole family have been making bets on who you would take after. I wish you knew your name. Your dad and I had a few picked out but wanted to make sure they fit your personality first. I wish I knew who you were, if you were my darling baby girl or my handsome little boy. We wanted to be surprised. Losing you wasn't the surprise we were expecting. I wish you got to see your room. And grow attached to a teddy bear that we would have had to buy 5 more of so you would always have one wherever you went. I wish I could have seen the incredible person I just know you would have grown up to be. I wish you had the chance to do all of those things. I wish the world could have known you. You could have done unbelievable things. Even now there is no doubt that you are still doing incredible things, somewhere.

I like to think that you're out there guiding others home to loving families, or that you are up there being looked after by the family members who passed on before you. Maybe your great-grandmother is up there reading you bedtime stories to help you sleep. Or maybe your Bampi is there teaching you all the shapes the stars make in the sky. Maybe you are one of those stars, looking down at us each night. Maybe you were the shooting star I wished on that night before the test was positive. Maybe you are in some fantastical place where lost things go and live happily ever after. I like to think that you are a superhero, that you are too great for this world and it is just not ready to receive the gifts you would bring just yet. If that was the reason you were taken from us, then maybe there is still hope that one day we will meet again.

I will always love you, all of us always have and always will love you. No matter where you are, part of us will always be with you. I hope that one day we will find our way back to one another and finally be together, our little family.

- Love Always, your Mummy x

When it rains look for rainbows, by Emma Geldenhuys

Content guidance: child loss.

-

When it rains, look for rainbows!

In the days after we lost Ellis, I found myself drawn to the internet, hoping to find people out there who'd been through what I had so I could see that they'd come out the other side. What I found was families who'd indeed gone through the same or similar, but who'd also managed to find the strength to have another child, something that I couldn't then fathom.

It took a long time and we really battled with our decision to try again for another baby after Ellis. Having struggled to conceive Ruby and being offered help with our fertility issues, I was adamant that unless I got offered the same tablets then I wasn't going to try. My thought process was that we'd had help conceiving Ruby and she came home, but Ellis was conceived without help from tablets and didn't. There was no way I was leaving this next baby up to chance, so I made an appointment with my GP. After explaining the situation she agreed that we could go ahead with the same fertility tablets, after running a few checks to make sure nothing had changed with either of us.

Even with the tablets I was nervous, I felt I needed this to work quickly to reassure me it was the right thing to do. Thankfully, I didn't have to wait long as after our first month on the tablets, I managed to conceive; enter a new wave of anxiety! I think I took a test weekly for about a month, and didn't tell Trevor (my husband) straight away. When I did tell Trevor he was delighted, but I must've stomped on his joy when I said "Let's not get our hopes up!" I felt awful as I saw his face switch from delight to fear.

I honestly don't remember much of this pregnancy; I've never enjoyed being pregnant and my sickness worsened each time, so I just took it day by day. I wanted to keep this pregnancy quiet for as long as possible, however when we did tell family and certain friends, I made it clear that it wasn't to be made a big deal of. It may sound awful, but inside I almost wanted to ignore it - it was my way of coping.

I was adamant that I didn't want to reach full term as this was when we lost Ellis, so I asked for the earliest c-section date. My consultant agreed to 38 weeks but it fell on a Saturday, so my c-section was booked for Monday 24th January, which meant I had to endure an anxiety-filled weekend before going in to have my baby. By Saturday afternoon my anxiety had skyrocketed, and I was convinced that I hadn't felt my baby move. I couldn't bear the anxiety anymore so I "popped to the shops", jumped in the car, and drove myself to the hospital. I needed to hear my baby's heartbeat.

I explained everything to the midwife at reception through tears rolling down my face and within seconds I was hooked up to a monitor and heard my baby's heartbeat! I rang my husband and explained the situation, and that the midwives had agreed I could stay overnight and even until Monday if I wanted. I was offered a private room away from other pregnant women, who I struggled to be around. Trevor brought me some overnight bits and said he'd come back tomorrow with Ruby so she could see me and hear the baby's heartbeat to keep her reassured.

On Monday as planned we were taken down to the theatre. The midwife instantly saw my fear, and knew I needed facts rather than irrelevant small-talk. Her voice was a constant in my ear telling me details of each part of the procedure, and before I knew it my baby boy was out and in my arms, alive! He was healthy, he was perfect, and most importantly he was going to come home.

My heart was so full and so broken all at once. Had Ellis been replaced? Would we have had Arthur if Ellis had lived? Would we forget about Ellis? Would I resent Arthur for not being Ellis? These questions are a constant in my mind. The truth is that none of them can be answered, and shouldn't be. Life dealt us a shitty hand and we're making the best of it. Was life easier with just one? Yes, maybe, no, life was certainly quieter, but the joy that Arthur has brought proves that having him was the right decision.

Ruby & Arthur have both allowed me to laugh again, and they've proven that life is worth living. Although our family will never be whole with Ellis gone, Ruby helps me keep him alive, Ellis keeps me focused on the important things in life, and Arthur has helped us heal and proves that the sun does indeed shine again.

Angels Passing, by Ruth Stevenson

Tales told

Laughter, sighs

Points made,

Scored and lost

Memories repainted

The long table littered with the remains of the day

We sit back and admire our wordwork

With bellies full

A lull

In the to and fro

From toasts to *tost*

A silence

One finds peace in it

Another words left unsaid

Looks exchange

Smiles

A roll of eyes

We wait, anticipate

It lasts a stretched second

'Angels passing.'

My grandmother's voice

Blessed are the peace breakers

The clatter of family resumes

Later, I wondered

What was she afraid we'd find in that silence

Perspective Shifts

Reflections on how our understanding

of ourselves and each other evolves

Firstborn, by Jessica Johnson

Shortlisted entry

-

I thought it was normal to feel so conflicted, triggered, and utterly devoted to your child. But then your baby brother came along, and showed me a new kind of love. One which is pure, simple and calm. I love you equally, even if admittedly it doesn't always feel that way, but the way the love manifests itself is as contrasting as you are from one another. Perhaps it's your opposed personalities which trigger different responses from me. You are energised, emotional and extremely physically affectionate. There is cheekiness there alongside your goodness, a constant potential to choose violence (mainly metaphorically, sometimes literally). Your brother is sweet, peaceful and observant, just like his daddy. He doesn't need a lot, just a book to look at, someone to hold his hand, and occasionally something to eat.

But you, my darling son, have always needed so much more. And so have I.

At night, I lie in a C-shape around him, wishing I could leave my bed and come to yours. Before he was born, we would bed share each night and I would feel at peace. We shared an innate connection, as if we were still one. Family would comment on how you were too attached to me, that I was creating problems further down the line, but I think that's what happens when you're a new mum figuring it out. I had no idea what I was doing, and so I tapped into what felt biologically right. Our days were spent breastfeeding and cuddling. Our emotions were synchronised, if you were having a bad day then so was I. You rejected anyone else who tried to soothe you. It's a little different now you are older, you love your daddy and all your grandparents, but when you wake up in the night from a bad dream it's only ever me you want. When you sleep next to your dad you are restless, limbs kicking and flailing in the night. When you creep into bed next to me, it's just stillness.

My love for you is fierce but so are my emotions and reactions around you. So much of what you do triggers me. I'm working through it one childhood memory at a time, but I yell far more than I ever thought I would. I have to constantly remind myself that you are only three years old, your behaviour is reasonable and normal, it is my job to regulate you and set calm and loving boundaries. But so many of our day-to-day encounters challenge me on a cellular level. You are my double, except you are unfiltered, untamed and have your daddy's blue eyes. He says 'I wouldn't have got away with that when I was his age' and I wonder when we became such cliches. I don't think I was like that at three either. We stare each other in the eye like opponents, knowing what effect we have on one another, but we are not equals in this. You are the child and I am the parent, and it's my responsibility to resolve it.

But then I look at your brother and I can't imagine ever feeling this way with him. He is seeing an edited version of me, a polished and corrected mama. Most of the kinks will have been worked out. My responses to him are warm, delicate and measured. When he cries it breaks my heart, but it doesn't make my mind implode. I don't go into fight or flight, I don't hear alarm bells, I just see my sad baby in front of me and want to soothe him. I'm not sure which one of you I feel more guilt towards. You, for the times rage and frustration has got the better of me, or your brother, who I don't seem to love in the same feral way.

I worry it will always be like this, our relationship will always be overflowing with love but sometimes volatile. What will the teenage years bring if we can't find a healthy equilibrium. Will your brother resent you for appearing as my favourite (I promise it's not true my love, I will write you your own letter one day to explain). Will your future partner bring me up in arguments, say you have mummy issues, say you need to work through your childhood so you don't pass it down to your own children. But maybe they will understand a bit better when they have a firstborn of their own.

You made me a mother, all of my firsts have been with you and yours with me. For the first year of your life we lived in our bubble and figured it out together. Birthing and raising you has been the rawest and most exposing experience of my life, destroying everything I thought I knew about myself. I wish you only saw the best of me, I wish I could be the steady and consistent parent you deserve. But I lie awake each night worrying about what damage I am doing in the meantime. Is your shyness and sensitive nature because of me? Have I passed it down through my genes or have you inherited it along the way?

I promise I'm trying my hardest, that's all you've ever deserved, you beautiful, brilliant little boy. So if trying, learning and an abundance of love is what our relationship is based on then I can only hope there are positives coming from it too. Positives for your brother, who will reap these rewards, and positives for you.

Somebody That I Used To Know, by Elaine Gregersen

You see me in the street, propelling him forward. The sun's bearing down. I'm sweating.

I pretend I don't hear you calling my name, until you clasp my arm gently and I can't run. My jeans have wormed down my hips, wider than they were the last time we spoke.

I'm angry. Angry that you went away. That you didn't visit, or ask how he was getting on, or how I was coping. Yes, he is very big now. Yes, I can't look you in the eye, you on your breezy Saturday outing. Yes, we were once close, but now we are not. I edge his wheelchair wheels along the pavement, like they're escaping for me.

How long has it been? you ask, whilst I stroke his hair. And I don't miss a beat and say four years. Four years since Prosecco O'Clock, 3am finishes, and text me when you get in goodbyes. Secrets spilling in toilet cubicles with giddy exhilaration. Dancefloors stuck to our soles. Weddings. Birthdays. That time you spent half the night trying to get free cigarettes off that bloke with the bad hair. Cake.

It's still your world, with your new friends and your new plans, the house warming parties and holidays. I sit in uncomfortable chairs in hospital waiting rooms and pour over educational psychologists' reports. I spend my spare time with paediatricians who talk about diagnoses and prognoses and ask if I have any support. At night, I race him to the Children's Emergency Department and watch doctors attach monitors to his toes and strap tubes into his nostrils.

I want to tell you that I'm still dancing. In the kitchen, I close my eyes and raise a shoulder up to my face, my head leaning to meet it, skin touching skin. I bend my body backwards and push out my stomach. I twist and contort, possessed by the music running through my body. Then, my phone lights up and I stop still, listening to scan results and medication changes instead.

I want to tell you how brilliant he is. How he's beaten the odds. How he sits with his arm linked with mine and by tightening his muscle a fraction he can tell me to take a spoon full of food and put it to his mouth. School sends home photographs of him standing, independently, clinging on to a plastic frame, his teaching assistant kneeling directly behind, arms raised out to her sides ready to catch. He is funny and full of personality. He whines when I put on the wrong television programme, but waits patiently, holding his hands in his lap, when we are queuing in a café with our two cheese scones.

I want to tell you that some days I am slowly immersing my body in a scalding bath. But my back slips down thick porcelain and more of me goes under. Belly, arms, breasts, neck. My head tips into the water and I can't hear anymore. I can't feel anything, except the steam in my lungs, the pressure and the panic. And I have to force myself up, to sit, and then out. Pins and needles swarm through my feet as I sway gently, feeling the lightness in my head, wondering if the hot air in my lungs will ignite me whole. It's still there when I sit on the bed wrapped in a towel, trying not to vomit. But you won't want to hear that.

I put on clothes and go outside into the world with him, my amazing boy, and I forget about what lies beneath. The grief. The lost dreams. The jealousy. But then I see you, in the street, on a sunny Saturday. My boiled skin slides off and I remember. I am not who I used to be.

Eclipse, by Joanna Bawa

She glides like a dancer across the room, this young, beautiful creature, pulling a ragged denim jacket on over the black vest with its fine line of sparkle. She is entirely careless of her loveliness, her youth, the firm smoothness of her limbs and the lustrous gloss of her hair. She frowns, searching for something, lines forming between her brows which will relax back into flawless skin the second she locates whatever is missing. Her slender fingers, topped with pink oval nails, flutter across surfaces, delve into her bag, her pockets, finally producing the object of her search – a phone, of course.

She taps at the phone, an expert interpreter of its pings and beeps, skilfully managing the barrage of messages, requests, comments and shared jokes that it yields in rapid succession. She is not only beautiful but popular too, the object of demand and desire, always forgiven for her eternal lateness because her presence never fails to brighten a room.

Soon she will leave, taking with her her sparkle and her joy, and this flurry of anticipation will swirl like snow then settle, melting back into the deep shadow of a Thursday evening. In her profile, her gestures and her voice there are moments when I see someone else. The way her hair curls a little more on the left than the right, which she hates. A narrow waist where her jeans gape, which will annoy her for years. The angle of her jaw, the flick of her eyebrow, the slight shrug as she deftly concludes one conversation on her phone and begins another.

All of this I recognise. None of this I will point out to her.

There is something so precious, so fragile about her oblivion. Others tell her she is beautiful, lovely, cute, but they mean, or she hears, only a detail. Maybe the earrings are extra sparkly. Perhaps the eyelashes are perfectly 'on point'. Or the tiny pimple fully concealed.

What she does not, cannot know is the vastness of her power, how her unsought brilliance casts everyone around her into darkness. I will leave this unsaid, because it would not make sense to her. She is not standing where I am standing, high on a pinnacle of years and experiences from where I can see what she cannot, that a tiny part of me has unfurled into this blazing, radiant creature whose presence is like a sun, leaving ashes in her wake.

How does it happen, this metamorphosis? The inevitability of blossoming, ripening, fading and declining, this inexorable dulling of hair, slackening of skin, thickening of waist and hip? There is a painful desire in me to compete, to show this gorgeous creature that everything she is came from, and remains, alive in me. If I did, she would smile and agree, she would acknowledge without any guile, that I too possess a kind of beauty. She would mean it in a way I do not, leaving me ashamed of my need to compare, my impulse to value things that are ephemeral rather than constant.

Lights glow at the front door as her lift arrives. She pockets her phone, pushes her hair back, turns her radiant smile on me. She is a star, moving across the night sky to fully occlude that other person, who has already dimmed and faded. She is entirely herself, everything that once was mine now blooming in her.

"Bye mum," she calls, "love you."

There is sadness in my smile, knowing that as she approaches her zenith I must move towards my nadir. Brilliant light fades to deep umbra, and, left in the shadow she casts, there is no denying that I am eclipsed. But not every part of me. Not my heart. That remains steady, high over the horizon, safe in its main sequence for a billion years to come.

I want to express this to her, to warn her, somehow, that the sunlight and shadows will keep moving, that this blaze of youth and beauty must diminish, unless, of course, over many long years, it is enriched by understanding and polished into a wisdom which will put forth its own steadfast beauty.

I want to say this, but she will know it is just the clucking of an old woman.

She hugs me and leaves, her life ahead of her.

"Enjoy," I call to the door, as it bangs shut behind her.

Second Child, by Claire Gough

I have to leave you screaming in the car
while I collect your brother from nursery.
I slam the door and keep my face level.

> I don't really hear what you say at the door,
> while I smile distractedly at Nicole.
> You want to play on the grass.
> 'Not today … dinner is waiting.'

Never blame anything on the new baby,
the books said.
It leaves a vague sense of things unexplained,
the gurgling elephant in the room.

Half-way through your feed I stop, leaving you
Unsatisfied again, to answer his shout
That he needs the potty, or he fell, or
spilled his drink.

> I play with one hand, smiling
> 'yes, sure, we can play that!'

And my joints complain as I stagger up
once more, or shuffle on my knees,
hands full
of sleep or feeding.

You needed sleep half an hour ago,
and it would have been easy then – but
I was rushing and playing and making snacks
and washing faces.
Your nails scratch your face from rubbing your eyes.

I can't hear what you're trying to tell me
over his tired cries;
Your frustrated hands clamp your ears.

I have to put you down to put my pyjamas on.
You are screaming, real tears squeezing out.

When he screams you scream;
Echo the baby with how new and hard this all is,
But it's too loud for me too.
'Stop it, now!'

I need to clean my teeth
I need to empty the dishwasher
I need to brush my hair
I need to pee

And you are left, complaining on the floor,
Away from safe arms.

And you are not heard, asking your questions,
Doubting my love.

As you whimper
against my chest
because I disappeared,
again, I whisper:

As you sob out the
feelings you
don't understand,
I whisper:

'It's ok; I'm here.'

The Mother Wound, by Kathy Giddins

At night I dream of all the things we left unsaid

Knife sharp cuts in the thread

Of our existence as

We scream at each other across the kitchen table

Unbound rage coursing through my veins

As it would if we were having it out in

The flesh and bones of my waking life

I once thought the waking life the "real" life

But now, having had dreams so raw and visceral that I
wake still steeped in the taste of them,

Drenched in the blood and the body of them,

I'm not so sure.

In my dreams I tell you "I don't miss you

Your name breeds apathy

We don't share telepathy

Although you live and breathe, you're dead to me,

Or, at least, the idea I had of you is."

In the dream world I'm bolder. Cut-throat. Succinct.

Don't tiptoe around it,

Or pirouette past your hurricanes like magic

In this realm, I shed the shame

Shelve the blame

Know I'm not wretched or selfish just because *you* called me those names

Unfettered by societal games

Don't think myself callous or wicked

For wishing you'd never been my mother at all

I excelled in spite of you

Survived the blight of you

Heart battered through and through

I love you

Yet ache from a cavernous void in the shape of you

My love for you does not dwell in the heart like love should do

It is a black panther patiently stalking the outer jungle of my psyche

And saccharin greetings cards could never articulate *my* reality

A complex tangled web of accusations, lies, hopes, expectations and hollow promises in their totality

A broken record

A narrative not spun by me, but a

Voracious politician

Indoctrinated by the party line you reaped to death

You're not my rock, my saviour, my confidant, or my friend

And if I could go back

I would skip to the end

Wouldn't stand back and take it

Like a deserter bravely facing the firing squad

Frozen to the spot

As you spat your venomous, vitriolic abuse

I wouldn't give second, third and chances infinity

Hoping that simply because you're my mother I could bypass the laws of insanity

At night I dream, and sleep unravels all the knots and gnarled brambles encasing my reverie

Things which during daylight hours just don't break through

Save for a stab of grief when I hear someone waxing lyrical about their mother magnificent

Or I see a woman pushing a blond curly-haired toddler on a park swing, so innocent

But at night all bets are off

Our story is a jumble sale

Pieces scattered about

A puzzling labyrinth

Fragmented parts of me scramble to make sense of it

Scraping the sad from the tragic

The love from the slag pit

Like dirt from a nail bed

A tailspin of regret

Sometimes things are better left unsaid.

Afterwards, by Simon Anthony Hobson

The first time I met her was at his funeral, the perfect tableau vivant of Southern European Catholic grief. She wore a black lace veil, hanky to the eye and sobbing, a tragic Madonna among the alabaster statues and niches with faded photos. The theatrical rituals of the funeral required me to shake her hand, the hand of a woman who was family but a stranger to me. His mother.

The afternoon sun glints through the Yew trees, casting witches' hats onto the Sienna coloured stone. The Italian cemetery, a morbid high-rise.

I move forward towards her, following the stilted protocol. "I'm so sorry for your loss" I say to her choking, almost overwhelmed, but trying to search for her eyes through the lace. I try to maintain a semi-serene poise. I am crumbling beneath. Her eyes dart at me in recognition, how could that be?

In a flash, she hisses sotto voce in heavily accented English "You will be hearing from my lawyer", flinty-eyed behind the tears while the coffin slid into the niche, my love letter off to an unknown destination. I am left reeling.

A month before, an unexpected drunken shunt and the car is rolling over downwards. We are helpless ragdolls in a spin cycle. I wake up in a sweat. He never woke up. A month has passed since the funeral and she is coming today. Apprehension lingers in the air. The sun is oppressive. The house is silent and almost empty. Any noise is amplified and I think I hear the faded echoes of past laughter.

The room is prepared, a premature mausoleum where

fragments of a finished life are laid out to be picked over. Carrion. The gentle lapping of the shore belies the incipient tension.

Her car stops decidedly outside, a slam followed by a confident knock at the door. I open the door determinedly. We face one another, stripped bare of any support except our own wills, eyeing one another up like polite pugilists.

"Please come in, I think you know the way" I say "I've prepared tea"

"Thank you", she says, impassively, in her immaculate Armani jacket. A woman on a mission, her make- up not quite hiding her drawn features. A calm surface but something ominous is lurking.
We go through to the sunlit lounge overlooking the becalmed sea and she sits down imperiously, almost

proprietary in her attitude but there is a slight wobble as one leg slides over the other and her bag is placed on the ground, just a veneer of steadiness I feel. I observe her, waiting. Small talk still prevails.

"He loved this view" I say, looking with his eyes. The sea witnesses this encounter as it witnessed our lives impassive with no opinion, not aware of the tsunami just metres from its shore.

The niceties are suddenly dispensed with.

"You know I knew all the time, don't you?" Her eyes are boring into me, I see accusations but also fear and sadness.

"Of course, I do. No one hoodwinks a mother. No lodger stays ten years" I try to lighten the already charged atmosphere with this last quip but the combat has begun.

I can sense her edging nearer her target, dancing round the ring waiting to land the final swing. Then she pounces:

"You have a month to leave!" A tumult of pent-up fury spills over.

"Of course, I should be out in a month, once the sale is complete", I say coolly, almost triumphantly.

In a split second, she visibly relaxes and then tenses, like a muscle suddenly pulled taut. Her eyes again betray her pursed mouth and stiff demeanour.

"This house is mine", she wrongly affirms.

"This house is in my name", I correct her.

Suddenly, she stands, furiously tapping at her phone and prowls out to the terrace where she frantically whispers.

She comes back in. Bowed but not beaten.
"My lawyer will check the paperwork".

"Of course," I say.

We are caught in a mechanical pas de deux, a dance macabre but the anguish is palpable.

She glances around the room as if she is looking for the first time, but her gaze is searching, almost predatory. I then remember she had visited on the days I went out. An occasional source of strife that I used to stifle with humour. "Don't forget to leave a dress out or something", I had used to shout as I slammed the door......

"I have packed almost everything but I have laid out some of his possessions in the study for you to choose"

We both walk to the study, this makeshift shrine, this grotesque grotto; the atmosphere is a foggy crackling mess. I am an automaton.

A row of polished shoes lies on the floor echoing dandiness but ultimate tragedy. His silver lighter, ever present, but its flame now suppressed and the comforting click silenced. His red passport, witness to a well-travelled life now permanently stalled.

Strips and dots of many ties awaiting a neck that will not be returning.

It all lies ready for inspection, unwittingly part of a choice that should never have to be made. She casts an eye like a hawk ready to swoop but, out of nowhere, there is an imperceptible change and a cavernous groan fills the room and she crumples to the floor, her bones becoming liquid, blind tears submerge us both. She holds onto me, not wanting to drown.

Devastation seeks solace in our mutual grief, silent, angry, unswaying and all consuming. I help her up as we cling to the flotsam that is our mutual support.
"I just can't, I'm so sorry" she blurts out in a muffled voice. Defeated, not by me, but by…. this.

So am I. Sorry for the moments she was not part of,

sorry for the laughter she has not heard, sorry for the complicity she never witnessed and sorry she never got to call me Simon. Sorry for all those things left unsaid.

Whispers of a Stepmother, by Tayla Kenyon

Things left unsaid.

Things that are not said.

Things that cannot be said.

Imagine being a mother without nine months of the year,

Without having to wait for them to get here,

Without the carrying, the kicking, the movement, the growing

Without the cravings, the mood swings, the '*oh my god, you're glowing!*'

No pushing, no panting, no sweating and shaking,

No stinging and ripping and parts of you breaking.

No excitement and build up to be a new mum

Never hearing the words '*look here it comes!*'

Imagine being a mother at the drop of a hat,

Becoming a mother, just like that.

The sacrifice, fatigue, and emotional strain,

The noise, the mess that drives you insane.

Feeling alone, left on the shelf,

For a child who looks at you with the eyes of someone else.

The child who was born from the womb of another,

The child who's the first to say, '*you're not my mother*.'

Constant reminders of a love from before, but -

'You can't complain, you know what you signed up for.'

Be a parent, a role model, an idol, a guide,

Chide yourself for your feelings inside.

Resentment, jealousy, times of despair

A mind that screams 'this just isn't fair.'

Put yourself behind you, for the sake of your man

Read blogs, watch videos, do all that you can.

Keep smiling and laughing through times that seem rough

Through daily reminders that you're never enough.

Allow the judgement and pressure to wash off you like water

Imagine this child is really your daughter.

Empty relationships; not for lack of trying

Nights of wishing, wondering, bouts of crying.

Sadness encroaching as your dreams start to fade

No first experiences, no *'look what we've made.'*

Is that all I am now – society's label?

A step mum? A villain? In my own fairytale?

Your feelings and thoughts now are all disapproved.

And how can you speak when your voice is removed?

To say this to you now; it fills me with dread

Things that cannot, are not, will never be said.

Mothers and Daughters, by Lucy Edmiston

I soak in the bath, bubbles lapping around the dome of my growing belly, composing a letter not intended to be sent.

Dear Mum,

We had both assumed that I wouldn't need to know about motherhood. I had thought there was nothing you could teach me that I couldn't find out for myself. And besides, my angry teenage claims that I would never be like you had probably signalled that being a parent was not an ambition we had shared. Until a change of heart at 38.

"Did your mum experience gestational diabetes?" the midwife had asked. The word 'mum' so unfamiliar now and surprising. It caught like a barb. Unable to answer, I considered my mother's mountainous shape. A body that had carried the weight of four children alone.

"Pre-eclampsia?" she prompted.

There was never any room for conversations like these. Our time was divided between avoidance or periodic clashing and name calling. Unlike you to miss an opportunity to centre yourself in sickness though.

The nurse ploughed on, biro hovering over my notes. "Difficult labour?"

Couldn't you have left me a note? Another note, I mean. 'Open in the event of pregnancy'. Neatly laying out the answers to these small, unexpected mysteries.

At just 24, no-one had prepped you with the answers either. No mother present to talk you through her own experiences and ready you for yours. She was absent for different reasons.

At the time, I would have been dormant inside you. Our future not yet unleashed.

The nurse continued: "Any history of miscarriage? Stillbirth?"

You had your hands full with four under five. Though there was a distinct

pregnancy-shaped gap between the first
two and the last.

It felt like a test I hadn't revised for. I sat there blankly waiting for the time to be up, until: "Any history of depression?"

Yes.

I knew the answer to this one.

There was a fusty smell of unbrushed teeth and round-the-clock bed clothes that sometimes permeated into the hallway. Days you spent in bed, curtains drawn, door ajar but unwelcoming. We foraged in the fridge for food, watched TV until past midnight, didn't go to school. The others asked me what was wrong with you. But I didn't know then.

A week later you'd emerge, butterfly-bright: "Let's go to the beach!" Grabbing towels and cozzies, buckets and spades. The others squealed, flapping about you with delight. No water or sun cream. I crawled around the house collecting those.

But I didn't say any of that.

The midwife breathed out steadily:

"Finally, who do you have to support you through this pregnancy? Partner? Mum?"

*

mothers and daughters and mothers and daughters and mothers and daughters and mothers and daughters and mothers and daughters *Dear mum,* drowning in the delirious white noise chant. the darkness. boobs loose and heavy. she's latched and gulping with unnatural hunger. milk trickles down and pools in my belly button. *Dear mum,* soundless sobs and unseen tears. drowning in the delirious white noise chant.

pins and needles in my nipples. this ferocious fatigue. my body. a spilled trifle on the bed. the slam of the front door punctuating the day; morning, evening. *Dear mum,* how i resent him/ his work/ his sleep. isolating day. isolating night. rocking and shushing and humiliated in a mess of blood and scars and tenderness. my contortionist cramps. my brambled mind.

Dear mum, mothers and daughters and mothers and daughters and mothers and daughters and mothers and daughters *Dear mum,* the long night. milking and crying. the delirious white noise chant. a new baby-shaped wedge between me and me. between him and me. my body, my heart, my mind. all detached. is it tomorrow yet? *Dear mum*, when does she turn against me? or do i turn against her?

*

I gently sweep crumbs and the flaccid rubber of a popped balloon into the dustpan and continue the unfinishable letter.

Dear Mum,

Parties were your specialty. A fifth birthday, not mine, was particularly memorable: kids ran riot, fuelled by the buttery, multi-coloured icing from a homemade cake. One boy vomited a rainbow on the pass-the-parcel and everyone cried, then their parents took them home.

Who were those parties really for? All the praise and commendations, confusing.

In the end, discarded party popper string hung like sad tentacles from the bannisters, and chocolate fingers crushed into the carpet during the musical statues' stampede remained as crumbly evidence. We lived in the debris for more than a week, eating sweets for breakfast and peeling shreds of wrapping paper from the soles of our sticky feet. Spent, you slept. Later to appear, raging at the mess that you had previously revelled in.

I remember how you panicked over invitations, not wanting anyone to be excluded and inviting everyone in the end. And their siblings. You stayed up until three piercing foil covered grapefruits with cocktail stick quills of cheese and pineapple. You cleaned the windows, inside and out. A pre-birthday spring clean. But I'd never seen you do the windows before. I tried to secure the bottom of the ladder with my bird-like eight-year-old weight, terrified you'd fall.

This birthday is quiet. Just the three of us, some sausage rolls and biscuits, a few presents and balloons. A fleeting, invasive thought suggests it's not celebratory enough. I watch my daughter draw in a mighty, determined breath and blow out the three small candles on the modest, shop-bought cake. And I flick that thought away.

The wrapping paper already in the bin, leftover party rings back in the packet, and cards displayed neatly on the mantelpiece. Soon we'll begin our bedtime routine of bath, story, bed. I'll tuck her in and kiss her goodnight and wonder what she wished for.

Constellations of Early Motherhood, by Finley-Rose Townsend

Mum,

I am writing to you from the future, thirty-four years exactly. Right now it's the eighties and you are just seventeen living alone in a council flat. The memory of that violent birth still swells inside your body yet here you are with a giant, beautiful lump of a baby to care for. You glance down at the list of instructions that your mother gave to you before she packed you off into that cold flat. A list that highlights the shallow depths of her own maternal capacity. But still, it's all you've ever known and all you have to guide you. So you follow it with scientific specificity.

1. Set alarm clock for every two hours.
2. Wake baby and change nappy before feeding.
3. Sit upright in chair to feed in order to prevent falling asleep.
4. Rinse nappies in bucket.
5. Stir nappy bucket every two hours.
6. Do not make eye contact with baby at night or whilst feeding.
7. Clean flat twice daily else The Social will take baby.
8. No biscuits or snacks, try to lose the baby weight as fast as you can.

I'm writing to let you know I see you. You see in this dozy space that me and my newborn son exist in, during the twilight hours, under the thickness of nightime, something in the space time continuum seems to blend and blur. And there you appear. I see you clear as day before me, seven years my junior, holding a scrunched up baby boy in one hand and a humongous terry towel in the other. I watch you fumble with the towel, begging it to form into a shape that vaguely resembles a diaper. I glance over at the pile of soft white muslin cloths that my husband pre-folded before bed and wince. Suddenly reminded of when we proudly told you "we're going to use cloth nappies!" and how you immediately began to rant about how difficult they were, how badly they smelt and what a waste of time it was. Dejected, I thought 'typical Mum always with the negative. Always has something to say. Always with some judgement.' Unknowing what visceral memories I had conjured for you of course. I didn't ask and you never said.

During these vulnerable and delicate moments of early motherhood, we've somehow slipped through a crack and fallen into the same time and space and here you are, in front of me now. I watch you startle awake and anxiously switch off the alarm that yells out, pulling you from much needed rest. I'm there with you, panicking as my milk comes in for the first time, leaving my breasts tingly and far too full to ensure a good latch. I search for anything to make me feel less alone, glancing over at his sleeping Dad I consider waking him for help. It would be simple to reach out my arm and tap him hard but wake him gently with a hushed 'Babe' and he'd be there for me. Armed with useless nipples of course but full to the brim of support. I consider this. Then you come back into focus, alone in that flat. Wrestling with that big, putrid nappy bucket in the hours where you should be sleeping, in the hours that should be spent being looked after, being cherished. An outstretched arm won't help you find a warm reception. You'd have to wander beyond the borders of your city to find someone to care. I decide to stick it out, in the dark of the night. In solidarity with you. If you can work it out, aged seventeen, alone, then I can too. I nod over to you, to let you know I'm here, letting you know I understand now. That we're in it together. I tell myself you can feel me in the ether.

Sitting up now and leaning forward, putting an uncomfortable amount of pressure on my pelvis I try to latch him again but he slips. I contort my wrist inwards to help flip my nipple up towards his nose. Off he slips again, crying out, frustrated and hungry. I've let him down. Before I know it I'm crying too. A feeble "I can't do this" escapes me. I don't want to speak it into existence but I've put it out there now. With each "I can't do this" I look outwards, searching for you in the dark the way he searches for me. The room swells and fizzes. This time I don't just see you, with my brother bundled into your arms. I see a hundred versions of you, whizzing past me, filling the room with constellations of early motherhood. Burping, crying, laughing, bouncing. I hone in on your stoic familiarity, allowing it to ground me. This time is different, you see me too. Eye Contact. A nod. Something within me settles abruptly. The room begins to slow, spinning to a halt as my body starts to tether. I keep on searching for you but you're gone now.

Alone again but connected I look down at those big brown eyes, the ones I am still learning. Gazing into his eyes reassures me that we're a team, then I notice it. I see his temple pulse and note the deep satisfying gulps. His eyes blink to close, seduced by sleep. Eventually slipping off, this time from gratification and I am overcome. I did it. I place him into bed beside me. We're both intoxicated, him by milk and me with my newfound confidence. He sinks into sleep and I decide I'll allow myself to do the same. Switching off the alarm on my phone, the one set to go off in thirty-minute intervals to check he was breathing. For I know now that I am in a silent contract with the women who came before me. They're out there and I trust them to watch over us both, as this sacred time and space belongs to us, Mum, it belongs to the mothers.

iykyk, by Ildikó Fritz

Content guidance: *allusions to birth trauma, child loss, mental health struggles, miscarriage, racism, sexual violence.*

-

Things are left unsaid when we talk, even though it sometimes feels like we do nothing *but* talk. We are women, after all; mostly, mainly, societally, for all intents and purposes. We're parents defined by our mammaries: moms, mamas, mommies, mums, mothers. We drink lattes and sip tea and eat sweet treats while we talk, talk, talk. We have been relegated to the outskirts; of society, of cities and towns. We have moved to suburbia or nice, walkable areas of town near nature and good schools and fancy grocery stores, because those are the things we prioritise now. We plan for our whole family now. We are vessels, wombs, bearers of fruit and nurturers. We are mums. We sit at tables in pricey cafés within walking distance from our homes with our babies in nursing scarves, strapped safely into strollers or to our chests and nurse our lattes and talk.

It's not all niceties, we talk of dangers and dark things too, we warn each other where we must. We choose the bear every time, and tell each other which men *are* (#notall). But we prefer to keep it light, palatable enough to go down smoothly with the lattes and sweet treats because we are not disruptors. We are the opposite of Chaos: we are Gaia, nurse mother to Zeus. We're the ones who rupture, the very fabric of the world is made up of our skirts and nursing scarves and we are not meant to tear and poke holes, we are meant to hold. That is what we do. Hold our children, hold space. Hold in place.

We leave the worst darknesses untold, leave them to stew while we make our family a nice well-balanced stew on the stovetop in our home and hearth in the nice, walkable part of town. We are mums, we are feeders, we give and we ladle onto plates, all the while keeping the unsaid inside, holding space for the darkness, holding it in its proper place. We *are* the proper place. We create the world from our bodies, we nurse gods and are hearths and hearts of our households. Our propriety is by default: dichotomy dictates to either madonna *or* whore. We are madonnas. The very fabric of the world can't get sullied. We clean and sweep, we wash away blood and fold wounds into place and speak soothing words while the things left unsaid accumulate inside of us. We sweep them under the rug, into the cracks of the floorboards, using Maggie Smith's poem as a manual. We're realtors showing houses of horror, building a beautiful world word by word on top of the kid in the Omelas hole. We don't dig too deep; we know that our nice homes balance atop boneyards. We keep it light, say the proper things. We are not supposed to tear at the fabric. Mostly, mainly, we don't.

Only sometimes do we slip up. Our mother's mouths fill up with the dark words, with the scary statistics, with the antisocial anecdotes. We talk about our tears and tears and show each other our wounds, slip down slippery slopes to subversive stories, tear further at what has already torn. But mostly we leave the unsaid unspoken. Held in its proper place.

We don't say: *this is dangerous*. We don't say: *no one in their right mind would do this voluntarily*. We don't talk about the mums who never bounce back. We don't say: *some of us remain incontinent, can't control our bowels, can't feel pleasure at all.* We don't talk about the babies who weren't born. We don't talk about lives shattered and children with needs so great that mothers become full-time carers. We don't say: *some of our burdens are unbearable*. We don't say: *I'm not fine, I'm not okay, I'm not able to do this anymore*. We especially don't talk about the mums that don't make it. Mums who abscond, leave, resign. Mums who fall apart in a foul way, out in the open, like an undressed wound. We're mums, not whores. We never, ever, *ever* talk about the mums who are whores.

After all, we're mums, not dads. Not holding it all in is not an option. Not for us. Our only remedy is talk. Talk, talk, talk. Supposedly it's cheap, but did anyone ever analyse the cost of housing the things left unsaid? Real estate is real pricey in our part of town. We talk to each other, to therapists, to counsellors, psychologists, teachers, coaches, preachers, healers, charlatans, psychics and all manner of doctors. We talk, but choose our words like expensive avocados in the fancy grocery store. We don't say: *an unreasonably large portion of my life is spent in the grocery store*, or if we do, we crack a joke in a caption – *it feels like I live here, haha!* – because we know we are lucky to live in a nice, walkable area of town with access to the good schools and fancy grocery stores, and we are grateful to be the mums who get to choose between avocados and throw away the brown ones. We don't say: *we are grateful not to be the other ones*. We absolutely don't say: *we are happy not to be the brown ones*. We never, ever say: *life feels like a zero-sum game where someone else's dead child means mine gets to live another day.*

We talk about how we love our children more than life. We don't say the other part: *I don't love or even like this life*. We let slip just a little darkness, just a tiny fold, a flag for the ones in the know. We speak in code, and put that in the caption too – *iykyk*. We don't have to say. We are mums; we all have the scars, the wounds, the folds, the untolds.

Afterword

'So long as you write what you wish to write, that is all that matters; and whether it matters for ages or only for hours, nobody can say.'
— Virginia Woolf, A Room of One's Own

Reading the entries to the Things Left Unsaid competition has been an eye-opening and deeply moving experience for all involved. As I read entries on the train, I found myself flitting between tears and laughter in an instant. The final piece in this collection, iykyk by Ildikó Fritz, encompasses some of the recurring themes: what is deemed palatable and unpalatable to say, the humour and darkness existing side by side, the pressure to perform, the huge societal injustices that shape all of our experiences to a greater or lesser extent. Thank you, to all those who entered - you have shared so much with us.

In book form, we hope your powerful words will reach more people. Hopefully just when they need them most. In the blur of early motherhood, reading what others had written about their experiences brought me enormous comfort. The knowing that others before me had given birth in different ways, breastfed or not, gone for months, years with broken sleep, and then sometimes done it all over again. The radical honesty often missing in our daily interactions can be validating and healing.

If this is where you are, now you've finished this wonderful book, I can recommend The Best Most Awful Job, edited by Katherine May, in which 20 writers share their beautiful, sometimes brutal experiences of motherhood. It was my naptime treat, as my cot-averse son slept on me.

Aside from the creativity and craft of the poetry and prose we received, the time and effort taken to write, edit and submit to a competition is not lost on me. When I opened Starcroft Farm Cabins, my two boys were under five and I wondered if I'd ever write anything longer than a sentence again, never mind writing to a brief or a deadline.

It wasn't exactly that there was no time. Even in those early days, my husband and I tried to give each other pockets of time to ourselves. It was more that I felt so simultaneously under and over stimulated, my brain so muddled, that I couldn't fathom settling down to write anything substantial. Instead, I sought fresh air and to reset. To appreciate the beauty of the world beyond my milk stained bedsheets. I was drawn to the rhythms of the garden. And I see now that as I sowed a wall of sweet peas and delighted in my bright, caterpillar-chomped dahlias, the seeds of stories were germinating too.

A book I continue to refer to is Wild Words by Nicole Gulotta. Her approach to a writer's life in seasons makes so much sense. Life is lived in stages, and our writing ebbs and flows with the years and our shifting circumstances. Our job is to embrace where we are. The season of raising young children, she says, calls us to be kind to ourselves and patient. Just as a child takes around nine months to grow in the womb, every story is birthed in time. We will have to rethink our rules around when and how we can write, and learn to do so in the margins of our days. A tired line in a diary at the end of the day counts. As does a paragraph scrawled in the nursery car park before pick-up. I found my phone notes were great for capturing sparks of inspiration or sporadic rememberings. Sometimes we won't manage a single word, and that's okay too. Our season to retreat will come.

Initially, the cabins were a practical solution to an issue many of us face. How can we fit work that sustains us around family life? A writer friend of mine, who visited shortly after we opened, said they were the biggest act of procrastination he'd seen. But as the noise at home grew louder, I like to think I was building what I knew I would need, and what you might need too - a place to write.

Living within walking distance of where the Battle of Hastings is said to have taken place in 1066, the most remembered date in British history, I wanted to illuminate lesser known stories. Having studied women's history at university, I named each cabin after a woman from local history. Not to adulate her in particular, but as a reminder that beyond the horrifying din of battle there have always been women whose lives and struggles have been forgotten. They may have been busy childbearing - William the Conqueror's wife Matilda, for instance, had at least nine children. Or they may have left written sources, but they've been overlooked. This was the case with Lucy Webster, who our 1920s cabin is named after. Her letters and travel diaries are there in the archives, yet the Battle Abbey heiress's colourful life has often been reduced to a single word in the history books: 'insane'.

Our three cosy cabins in Sussex now not only welcome writers from across the country - many of them women and mothers of all kinds - they have become my sanctuary too. As well as connecting me to a rich writing community, they're a place where I can escape the interruptions and distractions of domestic life. When I sit at a desk in one of the cabins, I have space to think as well as put words on the page. And surrounded by nature, the High Weald meadow, and the historic woods beyond, I feel at once grounded and somehow lighter.

And it's the doing it, I've realised, that matters. It doesn't need to be perfect, it doesn't even need to have a specific purpose. As Virginia Woolf, whose work is celebrated in our 1920s Lucy cabin, wrote, 'write what you wish to write, that is all that matters'. To express yourself, to process your feelings and your world, as the entrants to this competition have done. Regardless of the outcome, and whether or not you have an agent or a book deal. As my boys start school and I enter a new stage of motherhood, I'm revisiting Lucy Webster's story. I can't say whether it will ever be published, but I'm enjoying the process immensely.

It can be easy to feel as though our voices don't matter. And easier still to find something 'more important' that needs our attention. But as our writing coach Jo Norland says, far from taking away from family life, writing can make us better mothers. When our thoughts and words and ideas have not been suppressed, we can be more open to the joy and wonder around us. And by pursuing our passions, we show our children that they can too.

The tricky part is taking that first step, giving ourselves permission to write - we are the only ones who can do that. But once you commit, your efforts will be rewarded. Fatima, a novelist who came on one of our summer retreats, expressed a familiar sentiment among our guests when she said, 'It's been so restorative and transformative for me. It was my first time since being a mum that I had the time, space and quiet to really find flow again.'

It's such a joy to welcome Fran Hortop, who wrote the incredible winning entry, To the Undertoads, for an independent writing retreat. Time and space to ourselves, to create, is truly precious. Yet we hope she feels the connection to those who have been before, too. The women the cabins are inspired by, and those who have retreated in them. In each cabin we have a notebook where guests can leave a poem, something they've learnt, a message for the next guest, and in this way writers reach out to each other. They are saying, most profoundly - I am a writer, you are a writer.

So if you feel compelled to, write. Write around the edges of your day. Keep the spark alive by reading others' words. Take the pressure off, and just write because you want to. Because you need to, even if sometimes it feels hard. Continue to write the things left unsaid.

And if you find yourself in need of a retreat, we'll be here to offer a nurturing space where everyone's words are welcomed.

Hannah Stuart-Leach
Starcroft Farm Cabins

Resources and support

Discussion and journalling prompts

How has your perception of motherhood changed over time? What experiences have contributed to that shift?

Which aspects of the motherhood myth do you find most damaging? How might we begin to dismantle them in everyday conversations and culture?

What advice would you give to someone just starting their motherhood journey, based on what you've learned?

What does a supportive motherhood community look like to you? How can we create more space for honest conversations?

Reading recommendations

Lots has been written about motherhood. Below you'll find a list of books put together by Motherhood Uncensored and our contributing authors which have inspired, challenged and comforted us at various points on our various journeys.

1. *A Life's Work*, Rachel Cusk
2. *After the Storm: Postnatal Depression and the Utter Weirdness of New Motherhood*, Emma Jane Unsworth
3. *Bitch: What Does it Mean to be Female?* Lucy Cooke
4. *Don't Forget to Scream: Unspoken Truths About Motherhood*, Marianne Levy
5. *Inferno*, Catherine Cho
6. *Liberating Motherhood: Birthing the Purplestockings Movement*, Vanessa Olorenshaw
7. *Little Labours*, Rivka Galchen
8. *Making Sense of Motherhood*, Tina Miller

18. *Of Woman Born: Motherhood as Experience and Institution*, Adrienne Rich

19. *Shattered: Modern Motherhood and the Illusion of Equality*, Rebecca Asher

20. *The Republic of Motherhood*, Liz Berry

21. *Writing Motherhood: A Creative Anthology on Motherhood and Writing*, Carolyn Jess-Cooke

Support sources

One of the messages that comes through so clearly in this book is that the expectations, pressure and emotions that shape how we relate to motherhood are intense. This weighs heavily on lots of us and it's smart to seek help.

The contributors to this book have put together the following list of organisations who have helped us. Please do reach out to them rather than trying to struggle on alone.

Urgent help:
1. In potential cases of domestic violence or abuse if you think you, your children or someone you know might be in danger, contact the police.

For urgent help with your mental health, you can:

2. Contact your local GP surgery
3. Visit Accident & Emergency at your nearest hospital
4. Call the NHS on 111 and follow their advice here: nhs.uk/nhs-services/mental-health-services/where-to-get-urgent-help-for-mental-health/
5. Call Samaritans directly on 116 123 (Open 24/7) or email: jo@samaritans.org for a reply within 24 hours
6. Text "SHOUT" (or "YM" if you're under 19) to 85258 to start a confidential conversation with a trained Shout Volunteer (Open 24/7) giveusashout.org/
7. Call Papyrus Suicide Prevention directly on 0800 068 4141 (Open 24/7 for age 35 or under) - text / email also available. papyrus-uk.org/

8. Contact CALM on their national helpline: 0800 58 58 58 (5pm - midnight) - Whatsapp / Live Chat also available. thecalmzone.net/

9. Contact PANDAS who support anyone affected by perinatal mental illness - Whatsapp / call / email / support groups. pandasfoundation.org.uk/how-we-can-support-you/

Fertility, pregnancy and baby loss

10. The Fertility Network UK fertilitynetworkuk.org

11. Tommy's pregnancy and baby charity tommys.org/baby-loss-support

Postnatal support

12. PND Awareness and Support (PANDAS Foundation) pandasfoundation.org.uk

13. The Birth Trauma Association birthtraumaassociation.org/get-help-now

Breastfeeding

14. The Breastfeeding Network

breastfeedingnetwork.org.uk

15. You can read more about D-MER at d-mer.org/

Bereavement and illness

16. Cruse bereavement support cruse.org.uk/

17. Macmillan Cancer Support

macmillan.org.uk/cancer-information-and-support/get-help

Domestic violence and abuse

18. Refuge refuge.org.uk

19. Women's Aid womensaid.org.uk/information-support/

20. National Domestic Abuse Helpline 0808 2000 247 nationaldahelpline.org.uk/

About Motherhood Uncensored

Motherhood Uncensored was founded by Beverley Pannell in 2023 as a Charitable Association under the Charity Commission for England and Wales.

At Motherhood-Uncensored.org you will find poetry and prose written by people like you about the huge diversity of motherhood experiences that we often shy away from discussing. To accompany those stories and first-person accounts there are a range of expert interviews with academics, authors, medical professionals and activists on topics such as why postnatal depression is a feminist issue, systemic discrimination in obstetrics, the reality of health visiting, and flaws in our antenatal education.

If you are interested in sharing your own story, please do get in touch. You will find submission guidelines on our website.

Generations of women have asserted their courage on behalf of their own children and men, then on behalf of strangers, and finally for themselves.

Adrienne Rich, Of Woman Born

MOTHERHOOD
UNCENSORED

www.ingramcontent.com/pod-product-compliance
Ingram Content Group UK Ltd.
Pitfield, Milton Keynes, MK11 3LW, UK
UKHW022318120325
456179UK00002B/9